The Light from the Cauldron
I am Morgan La Fey.

The Light from the Cauldron
I am Morgan La Fey.

Joy Regina Melchezidek
with Morgan La Fey

For information on book sales contact: Joy Regina Melchezidek on Face book or email her at joyofunion@hotmail.com or call 717-439-8842 between noon and 7:00pm. est.

Printed in the U.S.A.

Cover Art: Suze Moll

Photo: Joy Melchezidek & Suze Moll

Layout and Design: Suze Moll, Roslyn McGrath, & Joy Melchezidek

Editing: Suze Moll, Roslyn McGrath, Judy Intrieri, Sandra Franklin, & Joy Regina Melchezidek

KDP-ISBN: 9798378721238

P3142023

This book is dedicated to the innocence
within all of Creation:

May the pure joy of Oneness be the
truth we live!

Also By Joy Regina Melchezidek

Kutumi the Cat with the Golden Eyes

Bridging Duality Through the Peace of Oneness

Acknowledgments

This book has been a journey of discovery. As with any book, many supported its creation. The following beautiful souls have Morgan's and my deepest love and gratitude for all they have done to help birth this book, so Morgan's voice can at last be heard:

Suze Moll, your encouragement, love, and honor of Morgan and me have held true to Morgan's message, whether creating our beautiful cover, working with all the left-brain techie expertise, impromptu edits, or layouts and design. Your time, energy, and beautiful heart have been pivotal in bringing Morgan's message to life, so beautifully and with such grace.

Roslyn McGrath, your continued presence, honor, love, and support of Morgan and me remains invaluable. From the beginning, you knew the importance of her message. Thank you for the hours you spent listening as Morgan's messages came through. Your keen eye for detail on the cover, your editing, your loving heart, and all the support you have given, helped to midwife this book with grace, and beauty.

Judy Intrieri, your time and energy with editing, your excitement and encouragement, have all added profoundly in bringing Morgan's messages into form. Revealing how she speaks in poetry, has given a clarity to her words that would have been missed. Much gratitude for your beautiful heart and the book angel who not only did her job but worked overtime as well.

Sandra Franklin, for your time and efforts with helpful edits, and the backup file. My gratitude for the encouragement to write you have given me over the years, as well as sharing the sweetness of your heart in the many ways you do.

To the moon sisters, Judy Intrieri, Denise Davis, Dorcas Eaken, Laura Danis, Shirley Mayes, and Laurie Woodward - thank you for your openness in receiving Morgan wisdoms and blessings. Thank you for your honor and love of her and for coming together and co-creating a circle that is powerful in love, honor, and Union. Morgan and I hold you close at heart and celebrate you each day.

To my soul brothers: TJ. Ryan, Rene, and Bruce, your support and encouragement were essential to Morgan's visibility and my completion of this book. Thank you for believing, and for your open hearts.

Kris Keirsey, my sister. For your excitement and support which touched my heart and encouraged me to stay open to the idea that Morgan touches people who might surprise me.

Nichole Bell, my niece, who confirmed Morgan's presence in our family, by telling me if Tommy was a girl, his name would have been Morgan Elizabeth.

Shannon Keirsey, my niece, who I can count on to give honest critiques and supportive input on my work. I love you all.

Special thanks to Pat Cowley, Wendi Greer, Melissa Middleton, Heidi Mary, Shoes Fillman, and Flo Magdalene for your faith, love, and encouragement. To Shari Brandt for your techie expertise and to all who offered support, my heart is full of gratitude and love.

Morgan La Fey, thank you for not giving up on me and reminding me that the magic is within. To our Fae, for the magic, love, sweetness, joy, and all you have done to bring about the completion of this book and the many blessings your presence brings to each day. To my book angel, what would I have ever done without you! To the children, for inspiring what is best in us all and shining so bright. You all have my heart. To the Source of all…. none of this would be possible without You!

TABLE OF CONTENTS

FORWARD

As a child, I knew little of fairy tales. I was busy surviving, as my life was filled with pain and suffering. It was an uncommon thing for me to play as children usually do. There was, most certainly, no time for fairy tales. Yet, at about eight years old, I woke one morning with a burning desire to write a play. Throughout the day, I wrote about the world being destroyed. This destruction pushed tree spirits and fairies underground so they could be safe. I made costumes from paper bags and organized the neighborhood children to play roles in telling the story. I was the producer, director, and lead actress. I danced in a tutu, while telling my part in song.

Shortly after, I was on a back forest road riding my bike, when someone tried to kidnap me. I was terrified of being outside or connecting with the earth. I didn't venture off into the woods for twenty-five years. I forgot the play that had come through me so magically. Yet Spirit stayed with me, attempting to awaken me and bring my memories to the surface.

I met Renya Rainbow Feather in 1995 at a spiritual event. A small sprite of a woman with dark hair and eyes, her wide smile and rich laughter caught my attention. When she spoke of fairies, I just knew she was on speaking terms with them. Opening the door to possibilities, I hoped to bond and communicate with them too. It didn't happen right away since my memories were held at bay.

When the movie *The Mists of Avalon* came out in 2001, I was spellbound watching it. It was as if I was remembering something precious that had been lost to me for so long. It quickly became a favorite.

My next adventure led me to attend an event that addressed the legend of Camelot. While there, I participated in an unusual ritual that involved a cauldron. Despite being uncomfortable, I felt compelled to enact my birth from the cauldron. "What an odd thing to do," I thought to myself.

Afterward, I took to the road, offering heart and soul sessions, classes, healings, and all manner of other metaphysical work. Of course, I forgot the "cauldron incident" just as I had the play from my childhood, until the year 2012.

During another spiritual event, I met a brunette beauty with a precious soul, Roslyn McGrath. Our connection quickly grew. I found in her heart a safe place where I could openly share. I was also writing a book about my life. With this combination of reflection and safety, my memories about the play surfaced. I realized as well; it was Morgan La Fey who told me the story I had made into a play. With Roslyn's encouragement, I allowed myself to open to Morgan and channel her. This marked the starting point of our deep communications.

I now share Morgan's wisdoms in soul readings, monthly moon classes, and classes with the fairies, Gaia, and Bridget. I have given channeled interviews on the "Joy of Union" and "Out There" podcasts, with my co-host, TJ Ryan.

In this book, Morgan's presence shows us magic exists even in times when it seems lost to us. Her truth-filled wisdom reveal her not as a myth but as a being of love who dissolves her vilification. She lifts the veil of illusion, allowing the light of the Goddess's womb, the cauldron, to shine freely once more.

Morgan and I offer you this book as a way to journey beyond the norm, into a world where magic is a blessing of Oneness that sparks the soul and returns your heart to home once more.

MORGAN OPENS TO THE LIGHT

12-6-2021   Midnight to 12:30p.m.

I am opening to the light, freeing myself from the dark places I once hid for safety's sake. Knowing I would travel many moons before resting in your heart, at last my voice is being heard. My voice is yours, spoken in truth underlining myths of days of yore. Had I known it would all surface so quickly, I would have spoken before, yet it is in this moment, I am called to speak of my early childhood.

Like my Mother Igraine, and her mother, from birth, my spiritual tutelage was the path of the Goddess. My foundation was strong, which prepared me for the difficult day to come.

Venturing beyond the castle walls caused me great fear of recrimination from both mother and my father Gorlois. It must be said that my family was with me in the confines of these walls. Truth was spoken in the telling of *The Mists of Avalon.* Not until Arthur was born, after my father's death and my mother's marriage to Uther Pendragon, would we horse play outside the castle. We would stroll through fields, gathering herbs and flowers for potions and teas of a medicinal purpose. Taking them home rewarded us with extra fruits at supper. Often, we sensed the Little People or the Fey as they watched us play.

It was thought by the towns people, that I was treated with privilege, as were many birthed in the castle. But both my mother, my father, and even my second father were stern in their care of me.

I was full of mischief and curiosity which I opened in my little brother, Arthur. We had a deep, everlasting bond which was nurtured by our adventures in nature, as well as in the secret rituals we emulated from what we witnessed at home.

MORGAN'S TWIN FLAME

12-7-21   12:15 a.m. to 12:37 a.m.

Arthur and I chose and were accorded the privilege of incarnating as siblings. In truth our bond was beyond the human connection of brother and sister. We were twin flames.

Arthur was closer to me than Merlin, Lance, or even my dear mother. Whether together or parted, his essence remained around me. We sensed each other with ease through a telepathic, empathic connection. It remained our secret always, until now.

Feathered bird wings were our symbol, heralding the news that the other was approaching. In days of yester-year, it was an easy feat to stumble across a trail or a path near the entrance of a forest or a terrene where these tokens lay. We'd gather the wings and prepare them, making them worthy of gifting to each other. Then we would compete to see who counted the most wings, coveting them as the most beloved.

I would eventually gather so many, I gave up my title and gifted my beloved Arthur a coat generous in warmth to be wrapped around him at his coronation. I loved him so, and desired that he never felt alone - not in his humanity, or in his divinity.

MORGAN'S VISION OF THE FUTURE KING

12-8-2021   8:50 p.m. to 9:10 p.m.

I am my words, or as you would say, I am in my words. In days of yester-year, messages flowed into my mind at such a rate and pace, penning them was nearly impossible. Thoughts quickened, tumbling one over another, leading me to forgo witnessing them on paper until now.

It was Arthur's swordsmanship that brought him first into the eye of others as having a king's capability. Others of our castle's heritage gathered around him when he was a young boy of seven. With little effort, he showed master skill at wielding a sword. It was proposed even then, as swords-manship was a requirement of a great king, that he was worthy of such a position. True, it was his destiny, making him even more fit to live the journey that was before him.

In his greatness, it was I who brought into balance his ego's expression of self-importance. At times he held himself in higher esteem because he was encouraged to do so. For nurturing him to be humble and countless other reasons, he cherished me. Many were the times; he would express his desire to rule honorably and with fairness. To assist his efforts to grow as thus, I would sit and witness his daily undertakings.

It was on such a day, with the sun high, and the day before us, Arthur challenged the townsmen to duels. Here the first vision of my dear Arthur came to me. In a victorious battle, he sat tall on his steed. The flags of both the God and Goddess flew with his surrounding army. I knew then he had come to unite the division that had grown between country and faith. On my honor, I pledged to support his mission, doing whatever it took for him to achieve his aim. I had no knowing to what I had agreed. I only knew the dedication my heart held for Arthur and the cause.

MORGAN AND ARTHUR'S SERVICE AND THEIR DEVASTATING PARTING

12-9-2021   8:05p.m. to 8:25p.m.

In my world, there were many causes that created great ambition for those of wealth and status. How corrupt they were defined their commitment to accomplishment evil deeds.

Arthur was a rare exception. Early on, he was our hope and our legacy, realized in years to come. Before our separation, he, with our trusted magician Merlin, and I with Aunt Vivianne, known as The Lady of the Lake, spoke of bettering our world. Always in soft voices, for fear of discovery, we shared ancient knowings. We planned what was to come but to some degree we were ignorant as to how our design would play out.

I loved the whole of my family but was not in a place of knowing how each would express their power with the intention of the betterment of our kingdom. Each had a role they clung to. This led to new probabilities as to its structure. So, it was decided by those who professed to know more how the concerns of power and who would hold a seat of authority, would unfold.

Later when Arthur and I were torn from each other, we feared that our soul twin connection would be lost. We were devastated. We suffered gravely. Yet, we were able to hold steadfast to our bond from the etheric plane, the place of invisibility, because we were practiced in our magical communications.

In Avalon, during my training, new powers were called to the surface. I was nurtured and under the tutelage of the high priestess, Aunt Viviane. This created an expansion in my abilities. Arthur and I teleported to each other, as we had in our early years but more frequently and with greater presence. Bridging the gaps between space and time was done secretly, for fear of being stopped if we were caught. We learned our lessons well and held true to our sacred bond as well our commitments to serving our higher purpose with pure intent.

MORGAN AND ARTHUR TIME TRAVEL INTO PARALLELING UNIVERSES

12-10-2021 11:30p.m. to 11:50p.m.

Our thoughts served as our words. Through time traveling we continued our adventures of growth and mischief. Our teachings allotted us new discoveries in this way of re-connecting. We were magicians, utilizing our power with wisdom. With deep regard for life, we honored our titles as Priest and Priestess.

We wore our robes as a badge of honor to complement our desire to be held in esteem and credibility as representatives of the God/Goddess. A moon marking on my spiritual center gave me a sense of pride at what I had accomplished during my sojourn within, as well as my teachings from Avalon. Outer garments appeared as a symbol of status and proclaimed the lineage of the Goddess. Dressed as thus, the world would view us as worthy to serve in petition to the Goddess. In this attire, we would be presented humbly and be received with honor and care.

MORGAN AND ARTHUR'S FAMILIARS

12-11-2021 5:05p.m. to 7:15p.m.

Having "the sight" early on, what was to come and who was to pass on was known to me. As this was a regular occurrence with all the women in my family, such was considered the norm. This gave me access to energies necessary to assist souls who were to pass to the other worlds.

Arthur's flying familiar was the Hawk, while mine was the Owl. Both were proficient with communicating in the dark, offering wisdom to the ready soul who made haste to heed what was being gifted. Owl, being my familiar, would present itself well before a soul responded to its yearning to leave the earthly realm. As it was a common bird in my place of dwelling, it was easy to see why I would covet Owl as my companion, it being the Hawk of the night and Arthur being my twin. It felt a true fit that our familiars were as they were. They were the power found in moonlit shadows which opened us to look deeper than a teacher would encourage us to go. Here we found every speck of light that was tucked away. Playing as children do, we pretended we were our familiars. We'd chased each other, attempting to capture the other.

With the caw of the hawk and the coo of the owl, we came to know that magic was afoot. Our worlds collided in a match that allowed visions of what was to come. We lived it all with childlike faith.

MORGAN TRAVELS TO AVALON

12-12-2021   5:00p.m. to 5:40p.m.

Knowing our time of separation was upon us, we shielded ourselves as best as we could, to soften the blow of our destiny. I so wanted my little brother Arthur to remain with me during our teachings. I wanted him to come to Avalon, but alas, the only trainees were of feminine. The isle would allow men to visit, but not to pursue their training there. Those of us learned in the old religion went to either Merlin or Vivianne, boys with Merlin and girls with Vivianne.

The mixing of sexual and spiritual energies were discouraged. There was power in both expressions, but the sexual energies were considered pristine, and for utilizing during love making at Beltane or marriage. Many Maiden Priestesses were in a period of curiosity concerning their sexuality when they came to Avalon. We were permitted minimal supervised contact with those of the male persuasion. This decree commanded that Arthur and I separate.

As a young maiden of twelve, I rode off with Vivianne and handed seven-year-old Arthur to our trusted Mystic Merlin. How I missed Arthur, but the busyness of each day kept me with barely enough time to let my thoughts wonder. This kept me from falling into despair. From time to time, Arthur would show himself to me in dreams and in parallels or we could step beyond the curtain of time. We would laugh once more, and all would be well. Knowing, our separation was an illusion kept me comforted.

I was fascinated by the rituals and the expansion of my powers. I was called a rainmaker because this was a craft in which I excelled. All the important days of my life thus far and with my passages in the years to come would be marked by the rains in all forms. I was fascinated by the mists, in that they were the protective element of Avalon, as they held an element of water. Trained to master all the other elemental expressions of magic--fire, air, earth--it was water that held the strongest link of my soul's expression for me.

MORGAN, MOON CHILD

12-13-2021   1:00a.m. to 1:30a.m.

A child of the moon, my connections were nurtured with the water of earth and the light of her most sacred sister, La Luna, or Selene the moon. Dancing under a new or full moon in the midnight hour with my once hidden friends, the Fae, I came to know them as my people and even as my children. For their mischief and magical ways of expression, I found them to be delightful and quite dedicated to me. Often, they were fearful, for many knew of the coming times where the old ways of the Goddess would be hidden and taken underground, giving them great concern for their fate. In my heart, I knew it was my place to take them under my care and guide them into safety when the need be. Their gratitude came to me in the form of entertainment, protection, and loving magic.

Trying to entice favors from the Nature God Pan, I learned to play the flute so I could accompany him. He saw me as his Priestess and Sister. I knew him to be my Brother Nature God. Vivianne would scold me as I was often discovering the magical ways of the earth kingdoms of which she lacked full understanding. We each carried our mark of the Goddess in ways that were individual yet compatible with one another. We were to express our own souls, not identical but complementary. Ultimately, we did so with mutual honor. This is the balance of the Goddess within.

MORGAN'S SOUL EXPRESSIONS

12-13-2021   7:00p.m. to 7:20p.m.

Of all, I was the most outspoken of my soul sisters in training. My lineage gave me access to knowledge and wisdom before coming to Avalon. What was out of the ordinary for them was natural for me. I found leadership to be quite a comfortable seat. Challenging my teachers was also a place that held little fear for me.

Vivianne both admired and abhorred my challenging of her. Answering questions that were never proposed to her didn't sit well in her heart. As my aunt, privately she laughed with me, telling me tales of our relations. She would mimic their ways, making light of them with heart humor.

In her light moods, she beckoned me to follow her under a full moon. Once there, the beating of frame drums held the rhythm as we stood in circle around a sacred fire. Our dance was that of the Goddess. With each beat, we stepped in rhythm with our hearts, all hearts, and the heart of Gaia herself. Beyond words, we were in a state of grace, bringing us all into a euphoric Oneness. I viewed each one as sister, with a mission to dance her purpose into being, just as I strived to do. With dance, there was joy in purpose and presence in joy. I loved how the Goddess would find Her home in my body with each move I made. Her name was mine at such times, for our union was a dance of Oneness.

MORGAN'S LIGHT AND CONNECTION

12-14-2021 10:45p.m. to 11:05p.m.

I came into my form, bright-eyed with knowing and light, and it remained so throughout my life. Keen in powers of discernment, as well being a seer and healer, it was so with my mother, as it was with her mother and those before her. In Avalon, powers unknown to me came forth. I uncovered not just a desire but a deep need to communicate with Mother Gaia. To me, her leaves in the autumn were as tresses of curls, falling from a full luxurious head of hairs finely woven into braided branches. Her waters flowed and whispered of days to come, where all the Earth would know paradise once more. Raven, steed, and hare were friendly in a manner which was unusual for even the likes of my kind. I would pause and hear Gaia's winds speak to my heart and knew her voice was directed by the truth of Creation. Her rumbling volcanoes foretold of a passion to release and recreate as the earth shook her tale into being.

Gaia's story poured forth from my cells, allowing me the honor of calling her sister, while making me privy to the secrets of Herstory and all that was to come.

MORGAN FEEDS BOTH PEOPLE AND FAE

12-14-2021 10:45p.m. to 11:05p.m.

In days of yore, the Roman Goddess Edesia held the seat of honor with food and its preparation. While at the kitchen ovens, I, once a pampered child who received her nourishments from servants, learned to bake an extraordinarily tasty herb bread. With the oil of olives, sage, rosemary, and a bit of thyme, I would take my fill and offer this manna to my sisters with a pride I had never known before. My preference remained to eat rather than cook or serve, but on occasion, I found joy in my culinary creations. Since our journeys were few, our sustenance grew on the island.

Often the Fae added touches of magic to assist the food growing process. If they were kept in thought and given a bit of sweet as a reward, they found it delightful to aid in whatever means they could, assisting in the care of all. They were fair in their request for a boon. Just as any who offers a service of quality is worthy of praise and appreciation. Our dear Fae deserves nothing less.

MORGAN REFLECTS ON THE POWER OF SILENCE

12-13-2021 6:20p.m. to 6:40p.m.

There were those of the sisterhood who took vows of silence and practiced with the dedication given to prayer. We have known silence as a powerful force, it being the language of the heart. The Egyptian Goddess Siege was known as the ancient etheric Grandmother who lit the night sky. Far beyond visible stars, her voice was never to be heard. Rather, through the silent whisper of knowing, her brilliance came forth in unspoken wisdoms.

In my devotion to the Great Mother, I gladly would have taken such a vow of silence and prayer. This was not my place, but I did fascinate over those who served in this way.

During the destruction of our temples and after, the sisterhood continued in convents. But alas, many nuns took vows of silence and were given second place in churches. The higher realms allowed this, lest the sacred sisterhood fall completely. I understood for a time, it would remain disguised as thus. Until the reemergence of the Goddess, when the status of union would at last be reclaimed.

MORGAN REVEALS THE TRUTH OF CHANGELINGS

1-15-2021 11:38p.m. to 11:58p.m.

The sun shown bright as the summer's heat brought sweat to my brow. Standing long in ritual, I called forth healings for the souls who found themselves lost in battle under the laws lacking in honor, giving little care to neglected children. Infant cries went untended as mothers of England were told, "No child shall be a proud soldier in later years, if he was coddled as a babe."

Husbands of those same mothers reinforced such atrocious laws. Rather than be fed and cleaned, the poor babes were to be hung in harnesses from ceilings 'til dry and kept there 'til their cries ceased. In grief, mothers would take the Wee Ones into the woods and leave them for the Fae to tend.

Many a newborn's spirit carried the essence of the Fae. The good folk would raise them with tenderness and care, seeing them as one of their own, for surely, they were.

Such is where the birth of this myth started. The innocent Fae were rumored of stealing children. Such awful recriminations for their kind deeds! Henceforth forevermore, the souls of all children came to Mother Gaia knowing of the love of our dear Fae. All receive a Fae visit before the age of speaking. Few remember.

The Fae are seen now, in the faces of the Wee Ones - the sparkle in the eyes, the dimpled cheeks, the point of the chin, and the cauliflower ears. These are just some of the ways to recognize the fairy spirit in a child. Creative expressions of dance, singing, poetry, sewing, painting and the like are to the Good Folks' credit. Creation Herself gives credence to the Spirits of those who had been held in captivity for too long. At last, the Fae dance in joy while lighting up the new world!

MORGAN'S REFLECTIONS ON HAPPINESS

12-16-2021   9:50p.m. to 10:10p.m.

Happiness in my world 'twas sorely different than ye could imagine. I reflected over a good marriage with babes and our very own castle or even cottage in the woods. Instead, I was whisked off to embrace the old ways as my mother before me, never having an inkling of being betrothed for many years to come.

Avalon afforded me quiet days, as well as the gift of sitting to sew. I loved to dress in full velvet skirts that gave warmth needed for rainy, frigid days. I managed to retain freedom of movement under many layers, as well as stay morally clothed. I braided yarn for knitting and loved embroidery. How I reveled in the magic of how tiny stitches could be used in decorating pillow shams as well as cloths for a table.

My little brother Arthur teased my prowess. He'd inject his humors vision of my future. I would laugh, "You have the good fortune to be family with those who could stitch a shirt as quickly as it could be torn in battle." It was a feeling of normalcy we played at, knowing full well we were destined for days when our purpose would lead to places unknown. We cherished the little time we spent playing in childhood and hoped that each day would last forever. How we wished we'd find happiness. Yet any happiness we were gifted was fleeting. For our purpose would lead us to choose service before joy, always.

MORGAN SPEAKS OF THE BELTANE RITUAL

12-17-18-2021   11:05p.m. to 11:25p.m.

My longing to be an honorable Priestess who utilized her magic for the service of the Goddess led to the choices I made. Not knowing history would call me a fable, proclaiming me a wicked priestess who destroyed Camelot, seemed to aid in how I lived with uncommon boldness.

My love of Camelot and dear Arthur called me to serve in righteous ways as well. It was all in the name of the Goddess. I was led to altars to petition the Goddess for assistance in honoring my calling for union of church and state with Arthur.

Even then, the holy wars were travesties, calling good people to revolt against each other. Seeing this as a child taught me lessons of wisdom beyond my years. In the days to come, I found my voice to be strong in its undertaking of causes near to my heart. Arthur, my mother, and many others who ruled did so with pure intent. We risked all to live our purposes with passion. We lived to give honor to the heart of this unified intention. To honor the same calling, to serve the good people. This was our walk. We held in our hearts a space for the other to live with integrity.

I had my future laid out before me long before I ever came into my mission with the Goddess. My calling was a decree and it led me to the Beltane Rites with Arthur, the future king of Camelot. Virgin and pure in our intention of service, we were eager to act the Beltane rights. We were led, quite naive but also curious, as to how we were to engage. Neither of us were free to keep company with our opposite.

To be allotted a night in the company of a young man was unheard of except under such rites or marriage. It must be said that what we could not speak with words, was said with our body's actions. Being of tender years and virgin, our actions were tender as well.

There was a familiar love between us. We continuously looked for ways to state our passion for each other. We did not recognize who we were to the other. We believed we were an impossible love and that would forever be parted after our one night of love during Beltane.

MORGAN'S VOW OF SILENCE

12-19-2021 6:22p.m. to 6:40p.m.

After the rites had been performed, the dreams came. It was always the same. A faceless lover with the mask of a horned stag adoring me in the only way he could. I was doubtful of any outcomes in our favor. Try as I might, I was at a loss of forgetting this lover of mine who was willed to me by the Gods, or so I thought.

After I was received in the Avalon order as a Priestess, I was eager to make my way back to Camelot. My longing to see and feel the love of my dear mother, and my little brother Arthur were my first yearning to be filled.

It was a day of celebration. Knowing my courses had not come did not dampen my spirit until I overheard Arthur telling our cousin about what occurred at Beltane. He was the lover that was assigned to me. Feeling devastated and betrayed by both Merlin and my Aunt Vivianne, I vowed then to stay silent about my condition.

MORGAN'S BETRAYER

12-20-2021 11:08p.m. to 11:30p.m.

Standing in a vacant hall, I cried silent tears for this love that could never be, and for the new life in me who would remain fatherless. It was here she found me, my aunt Morgues who was least favored sister of my mother. Feeling the betrayal of Vivianne and Merlin, I sought refuge and comfort in her heart.

With little encouragement, I told my sad tale of abandonment and betrayal. I wept in her arms, asking a vow of silence from her. To betray my unborn was a feat so horrendous to me, thoughts of Morgues breaking this trust never came to me. Nay, her betrayal was slower and more wicked.

Over years it unfolded. Her deviant plan to rob me of my child Mordred and kill him after his birth so she could claim the throne was altered. At Mordred's birth, she took him. She kept him in her care to gain his favor, all the while nurturing hatred in his heart for Arthur so he would kill him. In her plan they would claim the throne as king and queen. She imprinted his mind with hateful thoughts of me as well. She belittled my skill as a mother, breaking any maternal bond that might form. She taught my dearest son not to follow my lead or do anything that gave me influence over him.

Mothered by Morgues alone destroyed any chance of receiving love from Arthur or me. This was final in turning my son down a dark path, a path where kindness and love were as weaknesses. My heart yearned to love my precious one, but like Arthur, he was withheld from me. Would it be that my heart would know only sorrow and despair?

MORGAN BIRTHS MORDRED

12-21-2021   11:36p.m. to 11:56p.m.

I am Morgan La Fey, come to call on this Solstice eve. In my realm, the moon was high when winter's cold came to call on Solstice eve. I was heavy with child, ready to lay down my burden. Had I the strength to run, leaving all the world behind with its broken dreams and promises, with its illusion and forethought toward malice, I would have ridden to France. Nay, I was to birth a son who had no kingdom. He would be a king's secret son. I held this Wee One briefly and whispered my longing for his freedom before they whisked him from me. I prayed he be in esteem, with Arthur, his own father.

Here in my bed, feeling the desertion of my family, I felt more alone than ever. It was in this deep soul sadness; I was encouraged to take leave of my homeland. Torn between the need to care for my son and myself, I chose the latter. A six-week rest was funded by my aunt. "I will tend to the Babe. You be on your way in peace," encouraged my betrayer. Leaving my son and all I loved behind, I journeyed on my steed, with a six-pound bundle, to sustain me until our next meeting. With the wind to my face, and the cries of my newborn behind me, I rode off in solitude. Crying tears of grief, I let go of any hope of Arthur's return to me.

MORGAN'S HEALING JOURNEY

12-22-2021   4:40p.m. to 5:20p.m.

Much came to fruition on my journey. I communed with the Nature Kingdoms. Mother Gaia filled my weary soul with her blessings. Day after day, I traveled to the south where a warmer climate eventually broke free. The scent of wildflowers filled the air. I was privy to adorn my hair with my favorite blooms of wild roses. Through flowing, pristine waters, my thirst was quenched. Often my walks turned to silent reflection and prayer.

The comradery of the Nature Spirits brought both old and new beloved companions into my life, shielded me from harm, and aided the total care of my wellbeing. To be with them was more natural than not. I witnessed babes reaching for Nature Spirits as they smiled and giggled. Knowing that the Good Folk cared for the little ones with delight, filled me with peace. Whether I could see them with my eyes or not, I found them endearing. When not visible, I felt they must be off tending some service that required them to hold silence. When visible, I felt my world richer in love, as well as in magic. Walking under trees, they accorded me the company of their Guardianship. I felt their presence as protective and nurturing. It wasn't words that allotted us communication, but rather a deep sense of reverence from one to the other.

In the stillness of night, Mother Gaia revealed my purpose through standing on her beautiful earth. She remained steady, no matter what shifted or not, or which beloved was by my side. She was constant. For all her love, I found my loyalty to her was boundless. Birds wrapped in death, or a favored tree destroyed by lightning, found me weeping. As well, I'd rejoice in the birth of new life every spring. For here, I found the love of the Goddess expressed most joyfully, for us all.

MORGAN SHARES SOLSTICE

12-23-2021   4:45p.m. to 5:15p.m.

Winter Solstice or Yule was celebrated by both Pagans and Christians for a time, despite the split between the Goddess Way and the Way of the New King or God.

During such times, dance was part of our celebration. This delighted me, as it was my favorite expression of joy. As the world adapted to a God and began to diminish the importance of the Goddess, it seemed much of the magic of the light of our ways were dimming or being re-ordered. The misrepresentation of our ways deeply saddened me.

In my heart, the old ways were the way to peace and there the light with all its truth would reign. Our traditions were being reinvented to give glory and honor to the God, while dishonoring the Goddess. I saw the lie and how the people were surrendering to this new way.

It was not that I did not have a love for the Christed One. His way of love deeply touched my heart, but I found wandering away from the old ways frightening, and my need to keep safe caused me to challenge what was being birthed.

The adorning of trees in our nearby field made for a pleasant way to bridge the divide. For each path felt akin to the trees. The Christians honored the trees because of a belief that Christ was held on a tree to die. The path of the Goddess gave reverence to the tree spirit wisdom from the teachings of the Celtic ways.

Those of the Christian faith were more likely to peacefully feast, while gifting each other with delightful treasures. We loved to celebrate and make merry, professing this to be the gift - our joyous time together.

Harsh winters. would lead us to the fires and the joy of dance. Here we would find our spirits warmed by our joyous movements as the dancing flames would cast their warmth on all present.

MORGAN SPEAKS OF HER SON MORDRED

12-25-2021   Midnight to 12:30p.m.

Under the care of Aunt Morgues, Mordred was trained to lead and destroy. The heaviness of his closed heart was caused from the knowledge that he was fathered by a king and would never know the kingdom, nor his father's love, nor come into the safety and love of my heart.

He was feared but never honored by those who knew him. Mordred's army, knowing of his ambition to destroy Camelot, held him at arm's length when not in service. He was handsome and strong, yet he lacked a love to call his own. He spoke to love, calling it the enemy or weakness of man. He was empty of heart and with no recourse to free the passion of light from his soul. He drove his sword into the mighty and weak, laughing as a mad man. Seeing his soullessness, I feared for Camelot and all people who could be under his rule.

MORGAN SENDS MORDRED HOME

12-26-2021 5:15p.m. to 5:20p.m.

The web was woven and brought to pass. Mordred birthed the destruction of Camelot. This did not call his heart's truest longing to him. Later, when all deeds were done, and the war between father and son had been fought; I went to him.

My son, who barely knew of me, laid in my arms, his life fading, yet his eyes looked to me with a rare truth. There I saw his unveiled desire for the love of his mother. Beyond all else, I saw the spark of innocence that caused my heart to open to him the day I looked upon him for the first time.

With sadness, anger, regret, and love, I sat with him, knowing his spirit lessons needed to come to light. There he would find fulfillment in the great love of the Mother Goddess. I knew Mordred's lessons would cause him to return and he and I would look upon each other once again. But in that moment, I held him and gave him the mother's love he yearned for and told him, "Go to the light, Dearest."

MORGAN SPEAKS OF LANCELOT

12-27-2021   Midnight to 12:20p.m.

Being the son of Vivianne, Lancelot was my cousin. I still recall our day of meeting. It was in Avalon. Handsome, with the strength to challenge his Mother, he called feelings from me that I had never known. We weren't to be together, but a bond of friendship grew in the years to follow.

Twas Lancelot who still stood after Camelot fell. He knew of the death of my son and of the failing health of our beloved Arthur. Brave and true to his service of the Goddess, he would also fulfill the honors of giving Arthur the King's burial of which he was worthy.

But first, I and my little brother, the cherished King of Camelot, my Beltane Lover, would travel to the lake, in hopes of opening the mists, to enter the sacred space of Avalon once more.

MORGAN SENDS ARTHUR HOME

12-28-2021 10:36p.m. to 10:56p.m.

Setting sail on choppy waters, Arthur and I made our way to Avalon. The Lady of the Lake appeared to speak her warning in the roughness of the sea.

Feeling wrapped in a cloak of sadness, I watched as Arthur lay dying of the wound from Mordred's spear, with Excalibur by his side. With oars in hand, I attempted to give direction to our small vessel. Knowing Arthur was not long for this world, I prayed to both God and Goddess for the grace to usher my beloved home through the portals of Avalon.

Nearing the veil where I had parted the mists so many times before, I stood firm in my authority and I raised my arms, before bringing them down to my sides. The mist remained. Twice more I tried. Still there, we sat at the lake's edge with no movement towards Avalon. It was then Arthur handed me Excalibur saying, "Maybe Our Lady would like an offering."

Taking it, I threw the mighty sword into the lake. For a few moments, it suspended midair as if Our Lady was carefully weighing the worth of the gift, before receiving it. The veil lifted. It was the door Arthur's soul needed. "Go on to the Light. Well done, my Love." Tears fell from my eyes. I kissed his brow as he took his last breath. Hearing the flap of wings, I knew he flew home, and he was free.

MORGAN, LANCELOT, AND GWYNEVERE UNIFY IN HONOR OF ARTHUR

12-28-2021   7:00p.m. to 7:20p.m.

Standing silently united in our grief, Queen Gwynevere-the beloved wife of Arthur, Lancelot-his trusted servant and soul brother, and I watched as the funeral pyre returned Arthur to ashes. With him, he took Camelot. Yet, his death did not take the vision of Camelot from our hearts.

Gwynevere, compelled to give penitence for following her heart to the love of Lancelot while still married to Arthur, took vows in the Catholic nunnery. Lancelot, in deep loss of both the King and Queen to which he was so devoted, lived an itinerant life, traveling from town to town offering kindnesses, but keeping his heart concealed from any great love.

The Goddess would shine secretly, while the God would have his say. Knowing what was to be, the Fae found me. They followed me into hidden portals as the grand design would play itself out. But before I fled, I answered a call from my soul to journey our Beloved Gaia once more.

MORGAN'S FINAL VISIBLE JOURNEY

12-29-2021 5:37p.m. to 6:07p.m.

Before the warring and the fall of Camelot, there was peace in my heart. Called to live itinerant, traveling the land once more, I found myself reflective on my life's path thus far.

England, France, the moors in Ireland, and the castles in Scotland all recognized my Celtic heritage, my service to the Goddess, and the Pagan Path, even after Camelot's fall. Welcomed with open hearts by those who knew and practiced the old ways, I found great joy in the company I kept. Being in Oneness with my fellow sojourners on the path of our Mother, the majority called me Priestess and Sister Goddess. Others recognized my commission with the Fae and honored me with my title Morgan La Fey.

I wasn't in awe of my own presence, rather my service was done with deep gratitude and honor for all the magic and wonders the Goddess has shown me.

On my travels, the Fae accompanied me gifting me humor, protection, and magic as was needed with weather and sustenance.

In union with the Goddess, I traveled with only what my steed could comfortably carry. It was natural for magic to birth something from nothing. Living from my connection with Mother Gaia, it was a truth that tended to my total care as well. I was shown berries when hungry, and fresh water would be gifted from the drops of large leaves from the plants.

Winds would blow gently to cool me. When chilled, it seemed a blanket of sun rays would encircle me and give me warmth. Wolves would surround my camps lending protection when I looked for rest in caves.

In each place I was led, I tended the sick with the herbs from my satchel that been filled from the bounty of Avalon's gardens. How thrilled each person was to be gifted healing using such sacred herbs.

Other times, I would sit at a fire with the townspeople. While gazing at the flames, visions would come to offer direction to their days and peace to their troubled hearts. Knowing me as a light in their darkness, I knew them as those who would turn on me and call me sorceress one day soon. But there were moments I reveled in the joy of their company and the trust of their hearts, as well being honored as Mother of Magic to their Children.

My sojourn ended as I felt the drive to journey underground with the Fae. It was they who called me Mother La Fey. In the portal, I let go of the ways of man, as well as the betrayal that would be inflicted, a burden too heavy to bear.

Utilizing the magic I was so well versed in, helped me returned to my fairy troops. I assure them all was well, and we were together once more in peace.

MORGAN SPEAKS ON TRUTH AND THE SAFETY OF CONCEALMENT

My purpose required truth's accountability to separate facts from myth. Why so many myths? In the divide between the God and the Goddess, there were those invested in holding control, rather than calling truth a fact. For the sake of ease in the transition from Herstory to History, they bound what was truth with layers of lies and fables.

Through the division of the shift in power, the truth remained so bold, total destruction was impossible. So, much truth was concealed in fairytales. In my concern for the safety of the precious Fae, I could see the advantages of fairytale concealment. I allowed my name to be muddied, for the sake of those dear to my heart. I remained with the Fae until it was time to be brought to Gaia's surface and have our presence be known.

What did we do while underground, you ask? We hid in the brush and moss of the forests and teleported into a variety of portals. While in the center of the earth, we met the others. The Unknown Ones who knew the heart of the Underground Mother as substance and as home. We learned to let go of cares and worries. We knew our world would be as thus until the great change. At times, we would reveal ourselves to those who were ready for more truth than most. We could not let our presence be totally forgotten, for we had much to reveal and many truths to tell.

Hearing the echoes of the people's calls, over hundreds of years, I would respond by coming to the surface of Gaia. Although I was cloaked, a glimmer of my presence was sensed.

Leaving trinkets to spark the imagination, called more truth into the fables. Had no one risked for the good of all, the truth would have been forgotten. As a high priestess of Avalon, I was called to take this position whenever needed. Yet for so long, I yearned for the freedom our total reveal would offer.

MORGAN SPEAKS OF THE DIVINE

12-30-2021 9:45a.m. to 10:15a.m.

It was I who whispered to Joy of the Fae, the tree spirits, and the tales of days of yore, triggering her memories of the magical lifetime we all shared. I spoke how the Fae came under my care at the start of the destruction of the Goddess temples. I whispered how what appeared to be "death" was a temporary underground placement to keep them safe in my care. There was much death and destruction as the feminine path was laid to rest for two thousand years.

What remained was the masculine voice, his knowledge, his ways, and all the spirits who did his bidding. The angels took front stage, as the Fae went into safe keeping with me. I imprinted the earth with symbols and stones for those who had eyes to see. Much focus was kept on the Father's Son, Jesus. Many thought him to rebuke the old ways, yet he too walked a feminine path, honoring his Mother, the Divine One who birthed him.

He spoke to the Magdalene with equality in his honor and love for her. He required the same from his followers. I heard he and Magdalene were twin flames, each having the strength to support and uphold the space for the other.

It was Magdalene I related to. Her sufferings and strength in many ways were parallel to mine. I thought if there were to be a time we sat together; I would call her sister.

How exciting! Many came before me, bearing the face of the Goddess. How sad, all were held in judgment, ridicule, and disbelief. As did they, I tended my peace. I held strong in my intention that as a daughter of Camelot and Avalon, I did not lose my way in amnesia. I am in deep gratitude that while Arthur lived, he nor I, suffered from forgetting our truest Nature, that we, like all others, are Divine.

MORGAN HOLDS HER POWER

12-30-2021   6:45p.m. to 7:05p.m.

I have come to give testament. The mourning of the people, after Camelot fell with the death of my brother Arthur, left me with a heavy heart. Were I to enter into the convent with my Mother and Gwynevere, I would have lost my way and position with the Goddess. You see, I was not to deny Her, but rather to seek and to hold Her presence through the shifts of the times when the God would replace the path of the Goddess. I was to hold firm in knowing the truth. The Goddess could not be destroyed, no matter what temples fell.

I held silence, like a powerful weapon. It was in that stillness my visions came to me strongest. I could not betray my calling to Her, just as I could not betray my calling to my own soul. I was Her daughter, and she resided in my heart. She did not forsake us.

Rather she stepped aside, so that the God could come forward with his light and his knowledge to offer another way to peace.

Waiting in the shadows of the void, I was in Oneness with the Mother, knowing that the time would come to reemerge. During the time of destruction, I held firm to a knowing that restructuring would be revealed. I heard the horses and saw the fires that once celebrated the Goddess bringing to ashes the holiest of temples. I wept with my coven sisters, and I prayed with my Christian sisters for the rebirth to come quickly.

I knew the necessity of it all and yet wished that it were complete. When it became too heavy to walk Mother Gaia with my sorrow, I would enter the portal and find respite with my dear Fae. They would delight me with tales and songs as we shared mead and fruit cakes. How could I not find joy in such mirth? They showed me the newborns, they kept in safe care. I would giggle at their smiles and chatter. They filled me with joy, which gave me the strength to hold fast to my promise to the Goddess. In their eyes, I saw Her living on through them.

MORGAN SPEAKS OF THE GODDESS

12-30-2021 1:20p.m. to 1:45p.m.

I come to remind you, you too are one with She who is known as Goddess. In times of old, we honored Her. It was common for us to celebrate Her presence within us, as well those special times, Her holy days. I found Her essence in all of life, for in truth She is all. It was common for me to call her Mother and to allow communications with Her to flow freely.

I was one who spoke Her messages. As the old ways fell, Her wisdoms appeared to cease. As, the people felt without direction, I called for Her grace. Statues of Mother Mary were sculpted and recognized Her as the Mother of all.

Those considered of good faith, saw the Mother of Jesus as a good woman chosen by God, I saw the manifestation of the Goddess, offering grace and comfort. Knowing as I did, what was to come, I did not grumble about it. No, I gave thanks for this measure of grace that was afforded us by our Mother.

The biblical ways were branching out to all lands. Unlike the Goddess path, these tribes fought among themselves which seemed to betray the purpose of peace. Holding steady to my commitment to the Goddess, I felt a deepening of purpose, and more urgency to living Her path.

MORGAN'S WISDOMS ON MAGIC

12-31-2021   4:10p.m. to 4:30p.m.

In the days of yore, we came together in celebration to honor the shifting of times and seasons. So often, we looked for ways to find peace in the knowing of oracles, reading nature's messages, or sensing what was real or lost confusion in our dreams. There were adventures to be had in caves, but very often we would find relics that told of tales of which we wondered for eons. Then there was the absolute knowing of what truth was, as it gave us chills in our bones.

For me, the very the foundation of magic is founded in truth. Others would offer another view, stating magic is a quick shift to the hand, altering truth into illusion. Some call magic "miracles". With the passing of each day, you will come to know what I say. In choosing a course, we took our blessings in finding the middle ground of both.

MORGAN'S TRAINING IN AVALON

1-3-2022   12:12a.m. to 12:32a.m.

As a child, I sought counsel from others when I felt lost or confused. When I grew into a Priestess of Avalon, I was one from whom others sought counsel. Known for my wisdom of the old ways, I carried knowing of what lay ahead as well. Just as Merlin, I saw the potential in men's souls and heard the voices of truth that called in the highest purpose of God and Goddess.

The days of joy had come to call, or so thought I. What I was viewing were merely visions of times to come. In dreams, I saw odd representations of what would heal. I saw strange tools, ways of dressing, and patches with names. I saw sacred herbs pushed aside for the ingestions of medicinal pills, which was something unknown to me.

I often paralleled throughout my days. I was a time traveler, which afforded me the gift of going into future dimensions that previously were unknown to me. There I would witness the causes and resolutions for the divide between the God and Goddess. I knew I saw all so that I would take heed and understand the Mother's call.

You see, I was conflicted and confused as to why our Mother, would create a grand design that allowed Her sacred temples and teachings to be destroyed and burned. I was Her dedicated witness, sojourning from one temple to another. Seeing each torn to shreds or in piles of ashes, my heart broke. I cried tears for the Mother, myself, and all who suffered due to the recriminations of what appeared to be lost to us. In the songs to the new father king God, I found their voices sweet in their melodious expressions, and yet the tears I shed were those of loss and separation.

In my dreams, the Goddess bestowed Her grace on me, allowing me to feel Her hope of what was to come when I would travel into the future. With my mother, Vivianne, Merlin, Lancelot, and my Arthur passed on, I had few with whom to share my visions. Here is where the Fae kept me in company, reminding me that as high Priestess, I would continue to lay a foundation that would lead all into living the resolution.

MORGAN SPEAKS ON WAR AND PEACE

1-7-2022   2:15p.m. to 3:15p.m.

Around and around, we go. It seems the vessel of time has created confusion on the deepest levels for many. Wars were plenty in my time. Yet the desire for peace brought about the creation of Camelot. Arthur hadn't a knowing of how his passion for peace would play out in the years to come. The beginning of the destruction of the Goddess temples began with the birth of the Christed King. Its final shift came with the collapse of Camelot. Yet, its vision holds firm today. It represents the hope of a new world. It has inspired many to rule with fairness. President Kennedy, kings in England, and rulers of Celtic lands were also influenced by Camelot. Even all my relations who have passed on hold its vision in their hearts.

I was solitary in my practice, walking the sacred spaces we once dwelled. The Christian Soldiers believed their missions to be noble, and so I could not hate them. Nay, it was the pull of destruction that I hated, and how their laughter would intermingle with the crackling fire as they burnt altars. Repeatedly, I would find the place on Gaia calling for a respite from the heaviness that comes with war. In these spaces to release her burden of density, giving Gaia back the honoring that was so brutally snatched from her, I hid stones and sacred symbols, uplifting her aura and grids. Then witnessed as Gaia replenished Herself with the light that was offered. Her peace, gave me peace and Camelot came to life in me once more.

MORGAN SPEAKS OF THE BROTHERHOOD
BETWEEN ARTHUR AND LANCELOT

1-7-2022   11:00p.m. to 11:20p.m.

Often, I wondered how it all came to be, the illusion of separation, Camelot, Arthur, and me. From our early years, I was propelled to live quickly. Sensing our time was limited, I'd encourage Arthur, "Move ahead. Waste no time." He trusted me to hold the reins and would not question. Rather he'd strive to keep pace with me. No matter the action or interest, his interactions with me were very much of the endearing brother who I had always known and loved.

While ruling, his table was given a naive kind of trust, with hardly any forethought or discernment. This drew adoration as well as cause for concern. Those who loved him guarded him with their lives. Those who were to betray him played harsh with his heart, betraying his trust. Being of pure heart, he was shocked at finding ill intent in any. We who loved him, would rally around him, acting as protective shields.

The love between Lancelot and Guinevere was a Twin Flame love. Their love was as Arthur's and mine. Out of a deep love for Arthur, Lance denied himself stepping into the Queen's bed. We all held true to the service of the Goddess, while Camelot stood and even after its fall.

MORGAN'S QUESTION

1-9-2022   11:50p.m. to 12:20p.m.

Beyond time, it is all happening now. The past, the present, and the future. My time is your time. We are coming together to revere Camelot and Avalon. I have waited for this dawning to bring forth what is meant to surface and hold to the light what needs be seen. Thoughts of Camelot's demise never entered my consciousness. Along with Arthur, we held the vision of its promise in our hearts, pursuing our dream in waking moments by living its vision. We have come full circle, desiring to unite all souls. This place you call Heaven on Earth, I ask you now, is there room for our Camelot and our Avalon within your world? Will you allow the mystical continents of Atlantis and Lemuria to have room in your paradise? Will the drums of Mu beat for all to hear?

As the middle earth people, the ancient ones, the elementals, and all of Gaia's portals find visibility, will you welcome them home as they welcome you now? For this home, this heaven, this Camelot, this paradise, exists with the heart's warm welcome. Each one who came to call in my world, the warmth of our hearts held the door open to welcome them home. We of Camelot, along with all other worlds, extend our welcome to all. We choose to live peace, now. We call a truce from fear. We claim our temples of solace and freedom for all.

MORGAN SPEAKS OF CREATION

1-11-2022   10:55p.m. to 11:25p.m.

There is always more that needs be shared. From the seeds of destruction during the era of the Goddess, under the ashes and soot, lay the tattered, torn pieces of what was to remain to be brought forward in a beautiful mosaic hologram.

Reigniting the Goddess flame with the Source light, She brings clarity as to what remains and what is to be reordered. There is a place for the God as well. She is leading and is open, to receiving Him in Her cloak of Oneness. The secret, be it known, the true holder of power is the divine feminine. It is she who gives birth. In the womb of Mother Gaia's Ocean, a single cell creates something from nothing. The temples of Avalon held firm to this wisdom. She is whole unto Herself.

The ritual of Beltane occurred not to complete the Goddess but to give Her the joy of expressing Her wholeness through this act of love and passion with God. This coupling gave each the gift of remembering and expressing the passion of divinity together. From the Nothing which laid under the tattered remains of the destruction of Her temple lay the womb where all was possible. In His knowing of what is sacred, the God is received through desire which is joyful in its receptivity.

Rather than grasping from lack, many a woman of my long-gone days were encouraged to choose husbands from this space of need. Their fathers placed their worth according to the size of the dowry. This established a kind of thinking that woman were as livestock. Not so in the temples of Avalon. Here we were seen and exalted for our connection to the One and the priceless expressions that came from our hearts and souls. We would dance in ecstasy with our beloveds, rather than do a husband's bidding to keep us in comfort. A split between our desires of the heart and our needs of our bodies arose.

As the Goddess continues Her re-immersion into your time, She carries with Her the ancient wisdom and memory that dancing in the bliss of union with the Divine is inclusive of partnership and feeds all needs. This is the soul vision of the Goddess and what we remember. Choices made come not from the body's need but rather from the bliss of union.

MORGAN CLAIMS CAMELOT

1-15-2022   1:47a.m. to 2:07a.m.

So many times, in my reflections of what the future might bring, I envision my home, Camelot, as the paradise of peace that would branch out and inspire all lands. Had the difficulties of war caused me to question what might be played out differently? Why yes, I believed so, however briefly. Then I would go about my way making outlines inside castle walls that revealed designs for the future. Arthur, as well as the knights, engaged with me in creating these murals of peace.

Even Gwinn, as I fondly called Guinevere, would add a piece from time to time. When the days of trouble came, no more paintings or etchings were added to our dream of Camelot.

Instead, we began to conceal our blueprints with gray velvet curtains. When once we expressed the joy of what was to come, in its place we each held a silent sadness for what we feared we would lose. Our fear led to the conclusion we dreaded.

Surviving the death of my Arthur, my mother, my Father, and all the others, it felt like they took Camelot with them. I feared that I had I lost my home. Yet, as I pilgrimaged, I discovered that Camelot was not lost to me. Its vision lay in my heart as well as all hearts.

MORGAN SPEAKS HER TRUTH

1-17-2022   3:05p.m. to 3:30p.m.

Shortly before the clover came, I would wander the hills during those cool days. Just as the need to keep the blueprints of Camelot hidden felt necessary, I felt compelled to imprint my writings out in nature. Many of my writings have been buried or burned. Hoping to keep the wisdom of the Goddess concealed from the mistrusting masses, I resorted to imprinting symbols or writings in Gaelic.

Knowing that those who held the Goddess in their cells would understand, gave me great comfort. Just as henna tattooing boasted the accomplishments of the Amazon warrior tribes, so the symbols hold the truth of Herstory.

Soft-spoken, with the intensity of a gale wind, I was known as a voice of truth. When I tattooed symbols or sacred markings, this was seen as a valid expression by those who knew me. It would never occur to me to be less than the truth I am. Those who knew me knew this of me as well. So, look to your days and find now the truths of all manner that you seek. We truth tellers are here to speak. It is a time of revelation.

MORGAN'S BIRTH

1-18-2022   7:02p.m. to 7:30p.m.

The light shines brightest in the dark. This is where the Illumination needs to be. As shadows fall away, truth is seen for what it is. There are many moons in the cycle of dark nights, giving way to the light to cast shadows aside. It is so in the deepest walls of the soul. After the reveal of the dark night of the soul, there are truths to be told.

Traveling through my own darkness of self-questioning and loathing, due to the misguided judgements of others, I am gathering all of me from all dimensions as a visible, viable truth-teller of the Goddess. Many of Her faces are known. For the sake and necessity of the unfolding design, I dawdled in the shadows and allowed what needed to be played out to occur without interference.

In the silent times, my reflection mirrored itself in the dark pools of the void's fluids. Nurturing and basking in these vibrations of wholeness, I was held in the womb or Cauldron of the Mother. Birthed from this Cauldron, I ascended from Her womb as High Priestess and Crowned Mother Goddess to Fae. Gathering strength during this time of turmoil caused me to reflect on what the finality of the design might hold in these times. How I longed to hear the flute of Pan play in jubilation and listen to the rhythm of the frame drums that once found the heartbeat of Gaia. I wondered, were these times lost, or would they reemerge with the Goddess?

MORGAN'S HEALING TOUCH

1-19-2022   12:50p.m. to 1:15a.m.

I loved sweet cakes. Made from flour, the freshest eggs, and the honey of bees, the centers were stuffed with oranges, apples, or lemon, then sealed shut and baked over a high open fire. At times, cinnamon was added if the castle pantry was in supply. Sweet cakes were kept for feast days and celebration, but I thought nothing of breaking fasting laws and having a bake for those who were of hunger.

Our foods were in large part not only for our nurturing, but for our delight. I was known for creating simpler feasting dishes. Being limited in my abilities to cook, nonetheless, I wasn't shielded from the kitchen. My preparations of teas and tinctures gave me the title herbal healer. Teas made to taste and tinctures to heal. I would offer a mug of freshly brewed tea while applying healing balms for what ailed those who came to me.

For those suffering extreme pain, the tea wound be laced with an herb to distract and numb the pain. I would proceed without much difficulty in working the magic of healing. There are times I would rub my hands together and watch as cooling rays would wash over one with fever. Other times, I would hold my hand up, and it would be as if flames of warm healing would rush out to those who were chilled. In Oneness with the Divine, such times caused me to bask in deep gratitude for being a vessel of grace for those in need.

MORGAN BRIDGES "THE OLD AND NEW WAYS"

1-23-2022   1:42a.m. to 2:15a.m.

The old ways were known from that which was passed down from our ancestors. The new ways were formulated by the walk of the Christ Jesus. I was in distress watching the people give up our ancestor's wisdoms and magic to follow after Jesus. Yet I too loved his kindness of heart and his magical healing ways. Why could this not be inclusive? I would ask.

The ways were shifting rapidly. Even in my haste to respond to this quickening, I did not conform so easily as Arthur or the rest. I wouldn't cloak my charms that were tools for ritual, nor would I discard the herbal remedies, nor silence speaking of the sight. No, I practiced what was true to my heart, while honoring a choice many others were making, to walk the Christed way. It was here in this realization: I saw there would be a marriage. The God and Goddess would come together for the good of all. There would be no old ways nor new ways; they would merge into the way of Oneness. How my heart delighted in this knowing and yearned for its reveal. "There would be peace." I would remain a holder of this vision for it was my destiny to hold the Goddess's truth and all she gave me privy to.

MORGAN SHARES THE PURPOSE

FOR THE MYTH OF CAMELOT

1-27-2022 12:15p.m. to 1:40a.m.

A desire to see things from a higher perspective led me to study time travel and teleport into future portals. Arthur's sharing of his learnings gifted me this joy. Witchery was what some called it. Yet others knew how this would hold Camelot's place in the future design. Just as I received visions, I imparted them telepathically to those whose minds were open to receiving them, assuring Camelot would not be forgotten. For indeed it needed its place at the table of plenty, an inclusion in the heavenly earth.

So, I went about the business of teleporting into the future, imparting tokens of our riches in story books and fables. Here, fables were imprinted for children, offering Camelot in fantasy to them. Allowing our Kingdom to be remembered as myths and fables encouraged the children to seek in curiosity and in wonder, of what was this place, this Camelot.

I smiled in secret as I stood behind a cloak of invisibility in the shadows and watched the eyes of the innocents light up when they would hear of Merlin's magic and the strength of Arthur's sword, Excalibur. There was awe in hearing how our very own Lady of the Lake would call her treasures back to her until integrity would release these tools once more to be used for a higher cause.

Would that I had been witnessed even as a ghost and thrown off my invisibility cloak to be known by all. But the knowledge of my mere existence and the power of this truth-filled magic was not to be revealed until this present moment. For it is now! The end and the beginning are a circle that has long been awaited by the Goddess and the God of both miracles and magic.

MORGAN AWAKENS THOSE WHO SLUMBER-

HER LINEAGE LIVES ON

1-30-2022   2:30p.m. to 2:00p.m.

As I walked the land where my ancestors wandered and rooted their lives beyond the castle walls of Camelot, I took comfort and deep delight knowing the lineage of my people still existed in the DNA of their children.

In my knowing, I saw a time where the idea of Camelot's fable would cease, and the truth of its existence would be known through that lineage. Having gone so long in wait for this truth to be known and upheld in the framework of time has caused me to question the pace of the awakening. It's as if the herding of sheep had become an endless chore where gazing at the mountains on a walk had caused my soul to become weary. Had I lost my way in sadness? Now, the light has called renewed hope and purpose into me once more. In the thrill of Oneness, I see many of those sleeping sheep awakening to the vision of what was promised.

For now, we are walking together, and the heavy wool cloaks are falling away as the innocent spirits of those awakened Ones cast out the dense shadow of amnesia. It is my joy, pleasure, and honor to witness and shake up those in slumber. For as it is my time of reveal, so it is with all stepping beyond the shadows.

All are invited and you who have chosen to stay and live the vibration of Oneness are the givers and receivers of its gifts. More will be revealed as Mother Gaia's inner dwellings become known. In her, mysteries are resolutions the world is seeking will surface. For She is a living, breathing being, holding the secrets of many ancient lineages. In their recovery is her reveal.

MORGAN HONORS THE HOLY DAYS

AND WAYS OF THE GODDESS

2-2-2022 11:32p.m. to 11:55p.m.

I come before you, sharing my open heart. It was a yearly tradition, Imbolc, when we would celebrate the Bright One, triple fire Goddess Bridget, flowering her seed that would eventually call spring forward. This was the midpoint of winter solstice and spring equinox. Early morn, I would rise on this day and celebrate by drinking the ewe milk and creating a fire at dusk to give due honor to Bridget.

After Camelot's fall, I, a solitary devotee of the old ways, remained steadfast, upholding these truths on all the days that gave honor to the Goddess and Her ways. Truth be known, all our feast days were to be done in secret dwellings of caves or in silence at home. Recalling long-gone days of merry making, with music and dance, as well as the most delicious fare, my heart would be touched with both sadness for what was not and a yearning for the future to come. In gratitude, I upheld our practices not for memory's sake, but for reigniting our traditions for all.

Reflection has taught me those days of solitary celebrations were keeping the sacred holidays alive and giving sustenance to my own soul as well. As I continue my practice, I hold in my mind's eye the day all shall gather celebrating the Sacred Marriage and living the Oneness.

MORGAN SHARES THE PURPOSE OF IT ALL

2-4-2022   12:15a.m. to 12:45a.m.

I am here as part of the reality you are living at this moment. Opening to new worlds has called this my time to resurrect from days of old. In night dreams, you experience our connection in a way that would open you to seek and find this truth once more. I am she who you search for in the darkness of forgetting, and she who frees you in the memory of light once more.

Had your concerns not happened, our connection would have been lost. We are as one walking from the dark forests into the meadows where the sun reveals what is beautiful, kind, and magical. Have we not longed for freedom, or our souls' expressions, or our lights' expansions, as well? We are known to dance under the moon as the sun falls away. And yet new beginnings are giving us free movements under the sun's rays as well. For dancing in the daylight, we are revealed as the beauty we are.

Once hidden for the sake of agreements not of our hands, we are now free to choose differently. Hear the melodies of Pan's flute, Gaia's drumbeat, and flicker of the Fae's wings as they whisper hopes of new blooming. Listen to the drumming of the woodpecker and to the hum of the bee. Listen to the night owl and the morning dove. For all tell and sing a new song to usher the new earth's birthing. Listen and know that your time in the sun has begun.

MORGAN SHARES GRATITUDE FOR HER PURPOSE AND HONORS THOSE WHO SAW HER

2-5-2022   1:22a.m. to 1:45a.m.

Wandering in the hopeful days, of what might come, memories would be hard pressed, guiding me to what was needed. Had I known all would be wiped away like a beautiful dream, which was lost upon awakening, I would have savored each moment, creating more joys to recall when in the depth of sadness. How odd, after Camelot's fall, I would be the last to remain and the first to come forward for the glory of the birthing heaven, telling my unknown tale to open the light. Avalon prepared me well. I learned magic arts, elemental magic, healing with herbs, crystals, flowers, and waters. I became well-versed in trusting the sight that never failed.

My voice was strong in healing tones, and my gift of empathy laid a healing foundation for others. I became well versed in reading souls, very often long before they would come into realization with themselves. This kept me favored or feared. Those who were innocents, children, Fae, the creatures of Gaia, knew me as pure in my intent. Such is the mirror we encounter when gazing outwardly with inner eyes. I remain basked in gratitude for each who saw my light and knew me beyond the false judgements of men.

MORGAN STANDS FIRM IN HER POWER

2-7-2022   1:47a.m. to 2:00a.m.

My tale, though it may seem long and arduous, has validity in how I hold memories of finalities linked to the demise of Camelot and the knowings of the reemergence of the Goddess. Many stories have been told of how sacred temples and our Camelot were denigrated. I stand before you as a truth holder of memory. A spirit in form, able to provide knowings of what is truth and what is an illusions in tales.

Camelot was destroyed by the fires of rebellion much like Atlantis. Did the grand design require its total destruction? No, leveling to its foundation was not needed.

Standing witness in its fall, the grief lay heavy in my heart. But the light of knowing was to arise as the Phoenix from the ashes, and accompanied me into the present, affording me the gift of midwifery to this new world that you call home.

MORGAN SEARCHES HER SOUL

2-11-2022   1:57a.m. to 2:15a.m.

Beyond shadows, there is a light of knowing that draws me back to truth. In discovery of the demise of all the Goddess temples, I searched my heart, my soul, and with the Goddess Herself to uncover the purpose of it all so I would have peace.

What caused my dear son, to pick a sword against the Mother of all of Creation? Why would he be propelled to spew hatred against his very own father, Arthur, as well as the countrymen who could have led us from battle to peace? As a seer, it was known to me. He believed he served a just cause in acting as destroyer of Camelot. Although he was raised by an aunt of evil intent, he desired to love as much as to be loved. He believed he served something greater than man, and his pursuit of destruction would cause the fall to serve a higher purpose. In speaking truth, I say to you, this didn't erase the hatred of exclusion from the love of his father nor from his mother.

It was false, that he was birthed and deserted from hatred itself. I longed to teach him of the old ways and to bring him to Arthur for more tutelage in the ways of the Christed One. But we were denied this by my aunt and the souls' agreements between us. We were led to separate from each other with the intention of finding our way back together, taking the whole of humanity into union with us, this time.

MORGAN'S DELIGHT IN MORDRED'S

REINCARNATION

2-13-2022   15a.m. to 2:30a.m.

Many times, over the passing of days, I longed to make right what was due for Mordred. Any efforts to rear my son into the world through kindness, in privacy his acting mother thwarted. This made light of how my love would circle around him, too little too late.

In his time of his passing, I laid beside him, consoling us both with his head against my breast. I held him knowing we had only this, his birthing of spirit into form, and now, the passing of form into spirit. It was I, who cooed him home. I closed his eyes after his final glance of gratitude. I wept all the while from grief, regret, guilt, anger, and shame. He, my beautiful boy; come to destroy what the Goddess had longed to bring alive. What remained was a mere vision of paradise.

He was firm through hatred to be true to his piece in the design, just as Judas served Jesus in that design. My boy took on the hatred of those who longed for Camelot's vision to be fulfilled. Now, as it must be, he is reborn of flesh to be part of the newfound Camelot.

I herald the news with boundless joy. He surveys the land in the west, holding court with the Fae, for my dear boy is Fae by his soul's nature. My son, this time has come to shine. I am in the truth of my heart with great delight.

MORGAN'S JOY AND HOPE

2-14-2022 12:30 a.m. to 12:50a.m.

My hair was black as the midnight sky, and my eyes the color of green emeralds. They shone with the knowing of a Seer. Often my hair was braided with ribbons by hands of women who loved me. This lighthearted nurturing lifted my spirits.

Often, I'd wonder off to the fields and keep company with the Fae. They came with their flowered wreaths, crowning me with love and appreciation for all my undertakings. I'd place my feet in the cool streams, witnessing the Wee Water Sprites at play. I marveled at how they flittered about Camelot and its surrounding fields, spreading their joy filled lights, blessing all.

How I desired to call the people to witness their magical feats. I saw the Fae take sweet honey from hives, spread it over tops of flowers and welcome more bee visits, increasing hives and honey. They knew of Mother Gaia's ways. They listened to her, and honored her rhythms, teaching me to do the same.

Yet our Sweet Fae wished to stay invisible, seeming to practice for our future days, when we would be called underground. We would one day appear to vanish and become known as only a myth.

Yet in those moments, dancing water sprites shimmed and were illuminated by the sun's rays. If all could see such things, belief in magic would have been restored. Alas, all was withheld causing fear to grow and the magic of Oneness appear to be lost and with it the beauty of possibilities, became questioned. Until now.

MORGAN BECOMES VISIBLE

2-16-2022 10:05p.m. to 11:00p.m.

The Magdalene opened doors so the world could seek the way of the sacred union of the God and Goddess. The many names of the Mother Goddess came forth in a rushing wave of remembrance. Known only as a fable, my existence was questioned for hundreds of years. With the reemergence of the Goddess occurring, the possibility of my existence was on the table. Coming forth from the darkness of shadows into light, at last my light is free to shine. I am free to be seen. The Goddess's reemergence brought with it the challenge of breaking down the walls of judgment, shame, and invisibility. Magdalene's position of honor gave a new assessment of what was truth and what was illusion. In the division of the two points, I found my path illuminated by Oneness, as the tales of yesteryears brought forth new meaning. I knew what challenge I undertook being veiled for so long, as well as the rewards that came with the awakening of souls.

My existence heralds a louder call for the Fae from all Universes to come forth and aid in this new world. In their play, a lightness comes through, raising the frequency of creation, gifting higher vibrations to those who gave recognition and honor to these sweet ones. In their mischief making, belly laughs occur between troops. Being known as the illusions of nature and vilified as I was, gave us not only the common journey but such similar identities or states of being. It was impossible for us not to come forward together, for we are of the same ancient lineage.

Very often, it was my cloak that kept the Fae shielded from the human's eye and protected them from the harshest energies. They in turn called to my attention warnings as needed, when dealing with those of possible ill intent. We are a troop or a community. Our intent is to show the light of truth and to bring more love into the fields that were barren and only knew apathy. In the air one can hear the wakeup call that circles music through the mind, allowing the shield of sorrow and separation to fall away.

Some know these songs to be sung by angels, and yet we also have a song and a place in the choir now. Where the angelic songs are melodious and filled with beauty, there is a lilt or lightness in the music we bring. Spring will return soon. Not far off, the day of Beltane shall come once more, celebrating, and honoring the sacred marriage. It is with eternal hope for the lost that we open the door to invite the memory of the soul in each to enter and find its place in Gaia's paradise. Here we shall dance around the fires and under the moon, as the owl speaks, and the drums play, and the dance of creation has its freedom through the awakened hearts and souls.

MORGAN GIVES MORE MUSINGS ON WAR AND PEACE

2-25-2022 12:45a.m. to 1:30a.m.

The warring times in Camelot were few before the fall. Still, its imprint marked my soul, causing me to cry for peace from the depths of my being, holding true to this day. I, being a Priestess of the old ways, found it odd that travesties such as war would be used to seek resolutions to conflicts. Had I found on my path a way to source wars' conflicts, I would have allowed its nectar to pour from me like honey from a hive. Alas, my hands held the imprint of resolution's potential from the teachings of those who sat on steeds in battle. Those like my second father, my Arthur, and my brethren of the Round Table. I heard their counsel of each other and knew this to be a status they held in pride. Therefore, I held my longing for peace within, keeping it shielded from them and all others.

Our desire was one and the same, peace. Yet the journey was as two different branches on opposite sides of the same tree. They called for a war to bring about their means. I held outstretched arms to encircle all who wished to find that peace in sacred Oneness through the Sacred Marriage.

I recall this today, for in your world, there are more doors and ways to move out of war and live Oneness. Now is the time to beckon peace. Do not let disputes among men case you to question your heart and soul's knowing. Mark these words. The time of waiting has ended. So many have suffered with impatience through the endless days of war. Let not the illusion that has come to light cause you to question the soul's knowing. For the Mother and the Father have both designated now as the time of Peace.

Let this message hold firm and know that We stand with you in this ending as the birthing continues steady on her course. I am Morgan La Fey, and I bring to you this message of hope from my heart and from the very essence of my soul.

Now, I bid you adieu, for the night settles, and soon a new day rises bringing with it endless possibilities and hope's visions realized in the most unexpected places.

MORGAN SPEAKS ABOUT THE FAIRIES

3-20-2022   12:30p.m. to 1:40a.m.

In my care are the little Ones or Fae, who know me as Mother Fae. Their eyes sparkle from the light of their souls. How they illuminate with their smiles! Coming into human form has helped them be acceptable to others. You can see their unique cauliflower ears, and how their chins are often pointy. Then there are those dimpled cheeks!

Mischief and merry making through crafts, arts, music, dance, drama, and other creative expressions are the path of their souls. Unique preferences are often common, for there is little repetition in the magical dimensions.

The cap that was placed on the Fae preventing their freedom has come off, giving each bright One permission to live the joy that has long been withheld. Now there is wonder, life, magic, miracles, and the like. When you notice one with no tolerance for boredom, consider they may be a fairy figuring out how to live in a human form. Encourage them to continue with their play, for their energy will stay up and offer more light to herald in the awakening. You will see them hidden behind everyday work clothes. Many will deny who they are until they are caught in just the right light—the light of truth, the perfect place from which to open and to shine from.

MORGAN SPEAKS OF LOVE

3-4-2022 9:21p.m. to 10:00p.m.

I have come to speak with you of love. It is a weary soul who must wait for love's call. No need to tarry behind hopes and dreams of a starlit sky that shine forth from a lover's eyes. Rather look to your own soul, knowing its spark can ignite emerald, green forests of dreams from the awakened mind.

Circular expressions of spirals of lights, merging with creation's fire brings forth new life in the calling of desire. Tenderly in keeping with open hearts, Creation finds it's songs in melodious music of the soul. Love knows its own mirror in the eyes of the beloved. We are the fire of desire and the water that quenches its thirst.

Move on to destiny, never breaking stride from the focus of the heart's delight, bringing you into blue black-nights with starry lit skies or the radiance of golden shimmering daylight.

I have found my home here in this body, this temple, this divine vessel, and allow nothing but a lover's true call for union to know its delights.

MORGAN SPEAKS OF THE AWAKENING

3-8-2022   1:00a.m. to 1:30a.m.

Awakened Souls in their conscious flowering open each petal in their own time, remembering their mission to bloom. In days of yore, sitting in Avalon's garden of delight, proposing that the time would come quickly for this flowering to occur, knowing each life would be touched by the tender hands of the Goddess, giving it cause to bloom in Heaven's garden.

Delicious in fragrance, beautiful in artistic prose, winds would gently sway each budding beauty to teach it mobility in its moments. Oh, great souls, I know you to reside in this form.

Gardens of fluff and fun for the Fae to come into peaceful connection with the human were desired by these Fae. Knowing time would not lag caused them to prepare for a day when this entry would occur.

The heart of the Mother's inner world, my sweet Fae brought their play from the world above into the underworld. Finding warm water led them to fire parks that gave off heat as needed and whistling winds to cool the sweated brow. Here they never questioned longevity of age, but rather remained with the task at hand in the most lighthearted fashion possible.

In keeping with the vision's hope and its promise, all troops opened their hearts to the ancient Giants, the blue race, those that tumbled the soil, and all others of divine nature who found their peace nestled in Mother Gaia's heart. Knowing that home would arise for all, I knew also that day of awakening would come. That day is now.

MORGAN SPEAKS OF FREEDOM

3-15-2022   11:32p.m. to 11:55p.m.

It is I Morgan La Fey, coming to call in the still hours of the night. I tarry not during daylight, turning to and fro, accomplishing tasks at hand. Nay, I continue about the business of scattering my little Fay to go forth and play, sparking the world with their once hidden lights. "You are free. Now is the time of sharing. Nothing is to be spared or withheld from one's heart," I proclaim to all Fae.

"Priestess Mother, you call us forth and it is with great joy we deliver. For during this time of grace, our yearning for freedom is filled, and our waiting time is complete. We will speak to the fairytales of old and of Camelot, for its tale must be told but heard only in truth. As it fills ears, never more will He-Camelot, nor She-Avalon cry from death's tears, nor be bound by chains. Peace waves are settling in the bones of Avalon's tribes. The veil is lifted breaking curses. No one is regarded through the eyes of separation. Clear as the morning sunshine's light of truth, they shine. All are free from the shackles of forgetting and imprisonment of illusion's dreams at last. Eyes flutter wide open to catch a new day that has dawned."

MORGAN MIDWIFES FREEDOM FROM THE CAULDRON

3-21-2022   10:10p.m. to 10:25p.m.

I found you at the bottom of the well, or in the likeness of a Cauldron. Lost in tears of grief and anger, then there was that shame, making my breakthrough seeming impossible but imperative for us both. You could not see beyond your turmoil, while I could see beyond it all.

I have come to show you and them how breaking free from those chains of yesteryear offers another path home. Home, it is there in your body's heart and soul, in your form, in the temple.

The energetic Oneness wave continues for all eternally. For me, the freedom of movement in and out of dimensions is the equivalent to the soul's sojourn in your life, unencumbered by false roles serving only to hold the soul at bay. Hence the separation of the soul from the body has no footing with consciously living the design. Those days are long gone.

Setting your course for freedom, encourages you to step on the path of awakening, and claim your power. Please join me there so we may journey together.

MORGAN'S DEVOTION TO THE

GREAT MOTHER

3-28-2022   6:26p.m. to 7:20p.m.

Mother has many faces that She wears, and there is only She—the Great Mother. The one speaking would say "many are the ways She comes to us." If you give ears to my words, I will speak of our union now.

It was intended for me to live the calling of the Mother long before I recognized the Great Mother in me. I went about my days answering Her, paying attention to that still voice within, unaware of the full magnitude of the mission at hand. In childhood, I made light of the seriousness of the vows I had chosen. Partly being of such a young age and out of fear of the full responsibility of what was to come, I strived to make light of the heavy burden of purpose.

Arthur and I would mimic the serious matters and would voice exclamations we heard. How laughter filled us in our attempts at lightness'. We giggled a lot during such times.

As we matured in our age as well as our mission, we took our callings as seriously as we once did lightheartedly. It was then we would walk in fields of moonlit nights and conversed the occurrences of each day.

Arthur was trained in both the Goddess ways as well as the teachings of Christianity. Although I understood both I found my calling in the old ways, the ways of Mother. I found Her love everywhere. In the trees as soft songs played by the wind as She blew through the leaves. In the bees' hums as they expressed their delight in making the nectar of the Goddess. In the waters' whispers as, gentle waves moved over rocks in forest streams.

In the beating of the wings of creatures of flight. She was in everyone, everything, and everywhere. In the dance of tiny ladybugs who know just where to land to remind others of the wonder of nature's magic. In the spark of light in the eyes of all whether hungry, ill, wealthy, young, or old. Yes, I saw our Mothers' love in all I met.

In keeping with solitary company, it was my own memory of origin that filled the spaces in me and kept me moving forward in my soul's fashion. Gaia, held me in her womb every day. So, I shall tell you tales of how we agreed that Camelot must be created.

Hold still for now. Know tomorrow's awakening shall bring bright greater untold truths. For now, rest easy and know that the Mother is with Her children.

MORGAN TELLS OF AVALON'S BIRTH

3-29-2022   1:00a.m. to 2:15a.m.

First, I will speak on the birth of Avalon. It was but a seed in the memory of Creation—a future day to come. Before taking form, I sat in Our Mother's heart chamber knowing the plans of future happenings. Avalon was recognized as a sacred island, basking in the great Mother's womb. We witnessed as Her island seem to magically appear out of the mists. It was as if She was always there. Her Holy land would reappear with each parting of the mists. Avalon would renew her birthing ritual with each entry.

Her mission: to welcome those who chose to learn the old ways and live them. Her wisdoms are housed in the waters, the earth, the foliage, the trees, and all life. This is the blood that pulses through the heart of our beloved home. Many a soul who calls Avalon home has found difficulty in creating home in other lives. Their consciousness has held the question of the existence of home after the fall of Camelot. These souls often have roamed streets homeless and are held in little regard by all but seers of Light, until they remember the essence of who they are—their light.

Avalon's mists have hesitated to open. A protective shield is in place, holding off the density of those living in amnesia, until the awakened ones return to part the mists. Now, the great reveal is at hand, and with it the potential to gather is alive with possibilities.

When you come to call on the lands surrounding our Mother Island, step lightly and speak with the Fae of what you wish. Hold the hope that the water sprites will work their magic and that the veil of separation will lift once more, inviting all lost weary travelers who seek this paradise, which many call Avalon.

MORGAN TELLS OF CAMELOT'S BIRTH

4-4-2022   12:10p.m. to 12:40p.m.

In the same fashion that I experienced the birth of Avalon, I witnessed the birth of Camelot, whilst sitting in Mother's Heart Chambers. Avalon held, birthed, and nurtured the Divine Feminine. Camelot was called the earth's connection to the Divine Masculine. Side- by- side, they served, each known for the holiness of their own space and called to serve in a Divine capacity together.

As is with any sacred union, one cannot fulfill its purpose without all parts serving together. When Camelot fell, Avalon's mists of entry ceased to open. What remained in the hearts of men were the hauntings of a fairytale. Knowing how such beauty could be forgotten was too sad. In the fairy stories, even the saddest of tales, end with the hope of how Camelot lives on in the hearts of men.

Avalon went underground. There her portals gave us access to our island. Yet, the mist would not allow us entry. The areas where Camelot governed were accessible to all. However, few knew the holy ground they walked or better I should say, recalled the sacredness of our haven. The recall of the land and its location is now nearing. On this day, the mist will open, and the ground of Camelot shall rejoice in knowing that the sacred union of the land is revealed with all its mysteries and magic known. For this is a dimension many will call home.

MORGAN AND THE FAE FOUND THEIR HOME

4-10-2022   12:28am to 12:57am.

I recall riding my gray mare through the deep wooded forest in the night, striving to make my way safely whilst hearing the hooves of riders not far behind. Holding lit torches, they searched for me in thickets, in bushes of ivy, and in any other spaces that had potential to conceal me. Seeking refuge, I was drawn away from my beloved Camelot and all those who knew me.

My ways were now seen as corrupt by both those of the old and new ways, giving me cause to be veiled, not just for the sake of the design, but for my own safety as well.

Knowledge of the old ways taught me of portals in the forest. This afforded my access to timeless chambers by using the intent to merge with the energetic fields when raising my energy. My calling in Camelot and Avalon served me well. Both opened doorways for me to live my path with the utmost passion. One gave me roots and the other gave me my flight of purpose. After speaking to the wee Fae about the Middle Earth portals, I ushered them into hiding.

The littlest of the Fae, the babes, were confused as to why it was no longer safe to be seen. "Why must we hide away, Mother Fae?" they questioned. In my knowledge of what was to come, I spoke simplistically. "This will be for a time, until the people wake to a new dawn, a time of great love and community. Until then, we must prepare, but we shall be veiled and shielded by the "fairytales" to keep us safe. You, my precious Little Ones, will laugh and sing inside of Gaia's heart. You will come into more magic, through Middle Earth's people and the very rhythms of Gaia herself."

They seemed sated by this. As for me, the inner earth drew me to relinquish my suffering and form deeper bonds with those who knew of Avalon and of Camelot. We lived together in peace and were able to appear at will whenever necessary. Always, we returned to the safety of our new home knowing that She, the earth, would hold and nurture the deep-seated vision we held and were to grow in the awakening times.

MORGAN'S DREAMTIME GIFT

4-13-2022   7:07p.m. to 7:43p.m.

Each new moon, be it a howling wind, a rainy, snowy, or quiet eve, I send blessings of peace to enfold all while they sleep. Wishes are held in open hands and blown from my palms off into the night on sparkling silver rays of light, to welcome you each morning. I call on the Dream Weavers to aid in ushering magical blessings to all, asking also for clarity and assistance with your beautiful lives.

At the start, this ritual drew me into the Great Void. From my childhood days until present times, this has been my blessing for each of you and continues to be.

These early learnings caused me to open my soul to all and offer them an invitation to rest in this peace. Upon reflection, my gifting made known to me, it is there in childhood's joy that we discover our true vision of purpose.

During times of practicing silence, my comings and goings remained shielded even from my dear Arthur. This was one way I would midwife the inter-dimensions, assisting visions into form. This was a natural, solitary practice that came through me in delightful service.

It became common to find treasures that served as proof of success. The ceasing of tears that turned to radiant smiles on the faces of children as they looked upon me. When the angry rumblings of the earth grew calm, and the new food grew wild. When love was spoken. With each kind act, hope bloomed in my heart. In my yearning to extend peace it was and remains my highest desire to assist in filling each one with love and all the blessings of Oneness.

This gave witness to our paradise reclaiming and rebirthing herself. Arise! All you who sleep and live in falsehood. Camelot, Avalon, Lemuria, Atlantis, and Mu are just under foot—heaven has arrived for all who claim its gift.

MORGAN'S MOST TREASURED GIFT

4-15-2022   4:00p.m. to 4:35p.m.

Summer was a favorite time for me. The festivities that bloomed from spring, brought with them dance, minstrels, singing, sweet cakes, teas, and more.

The only dread was for the heaviest of clothing that was proper attire. In truth, it was my favorite season after spring. My birth being near the end of June also played well with Summer Equinox, for it was my celebration also.

Each year, Arthur would attempt to gift me a treasure more precious than the year before. His heart was my first treasure always, his handmade ivory combs for my hair, my second. "To decorate your crowning beauty, my sister of Soul and Priestess of Avalon," he said, smiling with delight.

Unknown to us both, this was his last gift to me before his death at the hands of our son. Hand-carved with the High Priestess symbol of the new moon in the center and a spattering of stars elsewhere, they were beautiful.

My dread was the memories of death would surface, as I wore the combs on the day of witnessing the deaths of both my beloved Arthur and our very own son. For his Viking burial, it was those treasured hair combs that I placed in his hands as they sent Arthur's body off to be honored through the ritual.

MORGAN SPEAKS OF HOLOGRAMS

4-26-2022   12:32p.m. to 1:11p.m.

Spoken words are part of a hologram, putting together pieces of a puzzle through vibrational sounds, creating future waves of conscious illusions or truths, depending on the teller. Those that choose to create and live beyond the illusion, or the sleep, will come forward to put the pieces of the puzzles in place 'til they fit.

Delighted with what comes from the beautiful mosaic of truth before them, they will be showered in the joy-filled expression of it. I, being a placeholder for the space of this construction, exercise my will as I please. Being as such, my existence was debated, causing me to question the worth of my expression for a time. Losing the chains of time, thereby gaining the remembrance of its completion, I no longer doubt my worthiness. For in the awakened state, all are divine and are free to express their divine nature. In my awakening, I find such pleasure in the mere knowing that my voice shall no longer be silenced.

In this thrill, I find song and heart's wisdom to be free to slip from my tongue as if the words spoken were first in creation.

MORGAN REFLECTS ON

CREATION'S GARDENS

4-26-2022   12:50p.m. to 1:10p.m.

To Luna's delight, beautiful, silvery moon rays bless the gardens who open their flowering faces before dawn. Sharing her shimmering light serves to nurture those blossoming even in times of darkness.

Our Mother reminds us, even in the darkest of times, the fertilization of life continues. Birthing Her beloveds before being seen and known in the light of day, who but Mother, could hold the containers for such magic?

The littlest fairies, who slumber long in daylight, can be found blowing on each petal under the Luna's softest light. Morning Star, Venus, in all her bright beautiful ways, will touch each flower after moving through the night, helping all to recall that each light has its purpose and blessing to share—none less than the other—each shining in the union of equality.

All gardens grow in the knowing that the magic of the old ways will make ready for such beauty to be the cloak on Gaia's body, each bloom being a jewel of priceless worth to welcome all into her heaven. And so it is.

MORGAN SPEAKS OF THE VOID OF SLEEP

5-25-2022   5:30p.m. to 6:00p.m.

I come before you to speak of nightly dreams. It is from there worlds are formed. From the unconscious mind to the conscious mind, I have found my way back and forth, from dreaming nights to wakeful days, to lay telepathic communication before each of you. It is there that I weave the web of foundation to assist you to come full circle in living your dreams fully in waking hours.

Here, I share my sacred stones to assist your nightly flights into the realms that open for you, so you may live out what has been accorded you. In nightly dreams, it is I who escort you, to join me in weaving the mastery of our adventures.

I answer a call to work in cooperation with the Ancient Dream Weavers. I am a Priestess Goddess who embodies the knowledge received from much tutelage in the realms of shadows. Here, the Light exists, even when it appears dark.

My wisdoms are well versed in dream times. When you recall a dream from asking that its wisdom be known to you, know that I have opened my heart to you to shine its light of truth, assisting you on your life journey. Within, lay all the answers to your questions, waiting for you to embrace them and fly free into the present. It is from the void of sleep that you birth your days.

MORGAN SPEAKS OF ONENESS

Deep in the crevasses of scabbing wounds, you will find my light circling in clockwise fashion, melting the hardened shell of fear, self-loathing, shame, guilt, humiliation, self-ridicule, self-doubt, self-harming, and the like.

It is in the forgetting of who you are, you lose your way, falling into the forgetting world, and residing in slumber rather than living who you are. So, the cycles of unknowing perpetrate into actions of discord, disharmony, and divide— the very things you loath.

I have come to you to speak kindly of the knowing of your soul, its essence, and of the truth you are. Before the forgetting times, the Source or Mother-Father God, and the experiment of multifaceted ways of expressing Itself came into being, all were one. All memories, wisdoms, ways of creating, of self-expansion, expression, and heavenly states of being, were known to all.

The experiment or birth of free will, caused the Source to split off, expressing and discovering Itself in countless ways.

All aspects of the God/Goddess agreed that this would be allowed, as did all souls who experienced individuation. The aim was for some to experience the illusion of separation from Source, with the hidden truth of Oneness tucked away in the soul. Upon death, a human would return to the heavenly frequency of Source and rest in the bliss of Oneness. A remembering of all of that was forgotten would envelop them and bring them home.

Death is not the only door to Oneness. Nay, raise your light in connection with your heart and soul. Here, I say to you, listen to the soul wisdom and the voices of your ancestors that speak truth. Hear the voices of the Truth Sayers and the Seers and of the prophets of old and now times. There is a dance of truth in the steps of walking the path of the Earth, the moon, the stars, the ethers, the youth, and the elders. Let its rhythm guide you.

I will continue to aid in the awakening, weaving away the ribbons of amnesia, which are wrapped around your cells. In your wakeful minds, hearts, and souls, know the essence of your memory houses the truth of oneness for you and all.

MORGAN'S MEDIUMSHIP WORK

5-30-2022   6:00p.m. to 6:20p.m.

I once walked the graves of the Ancient Ones. There I found solace from the noise of the living. Even before I sojourned to Avalon, I found fascination in such sacred spaces.

In the quiet, I would steady my heart and feel the spirits as they rallied round me in a fashion that would cause me to startle. In my recall of wise company I was keeping, I would find my way back to the stillness and take delight in knowing I was a trusted visitor.

On occasion, I would see spirits, and at other times, they remained cloaked from me, save for the knowing of my own heart or the gentlest touch on my shoulder or back.

In time, I would speak with them about the worries of my heart and know that they were not just mere spirits of the dead, but rather, they were as guardians, almost as angels, but not quite.

Though I knew them to walk the sacred space that I would visit, I knew they kept solitude near where their bones lay. For that was the way of tradition for many.

Still, I spoke to them of their freedom to fly into the light. At times, I'd witness the flight of a soul and note how it bowed its heads at me as if to give thanks for the heavenly invite. "Be on your way, my dear friend. The heavens, with our Mother Goddess, wait to welcome you!" I'd encourage. Those that remained, like me, witnessed the journey that took shape before us.

I, in deep gratitude for the knowings of their souls, blessed the ones who moved on and celebrated with the Ones who held fast to Mother Gaia in this sacred place. Here is where we continued to commune together under both moonless and moon filled nights, honoring the journey of life and death.

MORGAN HEALS THE PAIN OF SEPARATION

AND ITS SHAME

June- 5-2022   6:15p.m. to 6:35p.m.

I want to tell you that the juice of fruit eaten when ripe was my favorite gift from Gaia. Her gifts were plentiful in many forms, and my likings always led to the sensual nature of life— the kiss of the wind upon one's cheek, raindrops on a hot day, the smell of wisteria. All sweet, but sweeter still, was my love of the sweetness of blossomed fruit seed, to nourish the palate.

I suppose therein, lies a reasoning for quick judgment from those who knew little of me. Sensual delights were perceived as cardinal delights, where I knew them as gifts from the Mother of all of creation. The heavy judgment of the new Christian faith called for penitence, while my being celebrated in the sheer delight of knowing her gifts.

How I longed to embrace the world with my heart while gifting these treasures, but the timing was not, for waves of judgment lay a cloak of fear over the delights of Union.

All were given labels of judgements to ingest separation's shame. Dancing in the rain was seen as madness. Picking wildflowers became a trespassing of one's property. Picking the fruit off a tree could cause imprisonment.

New Christian laws extracted the freedom of expressing the sensual spiritual nature of the Mother, chastising all, laying a heavy shame on one's soul.

So, it was, and so it grew. Til at last, that very heaviness became too much to bear. Under such burden, the cries for grace came.

It was the Mother who heard. Responding to their pain, the women of no time or Oneness have come forward, breaking these chains so each soul is free at last. I too opened my heart, gifting each one with the sweetness of the Mother's blooming, without judgements of gluttony, but rather with a wish for one's palate's pure delights.

MORGAN'S GREATEST LEARNING

Had it not been the summer season of my life, or my early years, I would not have been privy to the allowance of free reign in the castle walls. In harsh weather I was kept inside the castle. While in warm weather, I was free to roam around a bit more. I knew them all, the maids, the horsemen, those who cooked and cared for us all, and their children.

Often taken from family and homes, younger servants were welcomed into the castle. Food, lodging, and warmth from cold nights were offered in barter. No, not a stipend in exchange for a kind or lovely service well done was offered, though our coffers were full. Yet we, the royal family, were known for our mercy and kindness. I would wander off on a touring and or an adventuring with all housemates, who smiled on me with good nature.

At times, mother and father would call out for me. Risking it all, I'd remain well tucked away, under the servant's bed or in the pantry of Cook's kitchen.

Upon Arthur's birth, it was the servants who gave me extra treats to reassure me of my worth. As Arthur grew, I gave him access to my play haven. All maids and man servants alike received my brother with open hearts, yet they remained loyal to our already-formed bonds.

"Arthur, make haste! Morgan calls for you. In your play, remember it is she who needs to be heard by you. She will tally naught when you are in need. Rather, be loyal to her directions and know our Morgan will not lead you astray." I would hear their honor for me and felt it touch my heart in the way of love.

Such kindness caused me to hold my position as one of worth and value, even after a future King was born. Here I found roots to honor my own heart and soul.

Later in Avalon, I would learn of the honor that the kingdoms held for me. Yet the wisdom of my early days stayed with me. "I must serve humbly to be of any true service," I would require of myself. There in the castle kitchen and under the watchful eyes of servants, I learned my first important teaching, humility, and I am grateful.

MORGAN SPEAKS Of CAMELOT'S
GOVERNMENT

6-272022   7:10p.m. to 7:50p.m.

In days of yore, the governing laws would be defined "harsh" according to your world. Yet the harshness suited the crime for the Goddess rules with a strong, compassionate heart, and an all-knowing consciousness. Her fairness taught lessons more than gave reprimands.

She honored all, people, animals, nature, the earth. All were treated fairly. With Her seed in our essence, I knew destruction of life in any form was an attempt to destroy Her. From the depth of my being, I could not and would not tolerate such treatment of our Divine Mother.

My early days were the ways of the Mother. Her wisdoms were honored, and Her counsel served in pure intent. I witnessed as Her ways were disregarded for a time Her words ceased. I felt Her tears. I knew there would come a time, when they would be the water to nurture a new way, a time of great awakening. So, it is now. Rise and unite men, women, and children! Remember, the time of lies and truth are upon everyone. The path you live is what you nurture. Know this for those who have ears to hear. It is the time of awakening.

MORGAN SPEAKS OF LOSS AND
WHAT IS SACRED

7-10-2022   5:40p.m. to 6:05p.m.

Flowers, herbs, and cauldrons—they called these "witchy things" after hundreds of years of purpose. In my realms, they were gifts of the Mother. Scents and potions were medicinal. Flowers and leaves adorned crowns of Gods, Goddesses and newborn royalty, giving honor to their presence. Lucious soaks for kings and queens provided refreshment, as well a bit of rest from a long day. Basking in Lavendar, healed headaches and sleeplessness. Savory aromas from soup and stew cauldrons caused a watering pallet and a grumbling belly.

I never foresaw a day my cauldron would be removed. "Take them away. Remove the walking sticks, as you see its power symbols reveal a use for more than walking." What were once common necessities were ordained as evil objects. Henceforth, I hid my treasures in wooded areas, knowing that the Fae would keep them safe. Now I See cauldrons, potions, teas, and lotions proudly displayed. Yet, once again, those who seem to be wearing authority are calling for the removal of feminine empowerment. Rest assured, these days have been preordained to be the days of the Sacred Marriage, the coming together of all ages. There will be minimal time for illusion's tale to weave any issue of denigration. Worry not, for these are days of new birthing and true freedoms.

MORGAN SPEAKS OF MOTHER EARTH'S LOVE

7-11-2022   6:15p.m. to 6:45p.m.

Stepping lightly from the portals or doorways of the Middle Earth, I discover, uncover, and rediscover my whereabouts once more. In days of old, being privy to living on Gaia or our Mother Earth, I would wander about aimlessly, never knowing that my days on her would be limited. Taking this privilege so lightly, never caused fear nor concern. I knew shifts were coming. What caused me distress later was my lack of awareness and presence with knowing that the earth was shifting along with all else. Here I learned that Gaia and her will have been part of the hidden equation of the evolution of all. Coming into the present, I marvel over her new flow. Many are creating new ways of being or creating new systems designed to support living heaven on earth. Holding the codes of creation, both ancient and newfound wisdoms are known to me. I offer warnings of what can cause unnecessary harm to our Earth and to her people.

I am also called to bring wisdoms, offering support to assist with a more graceful birthing for all. What is the same from then to now, you might ask? I say that Mother Earth nurtures what life forms remain, while designing new life forms as needed. Herein, she expresses her flow with Creation's frequency, expanding outwardly in waves. Each and every creation has its own beauty, to be honored and valued as all are worthy. This is her message to us. Creation honors and cherishes us. Such is the nature of her love. It is timeless, as are we.

223

MORGAN SPEAKS OF THE GODDESS AND THE PROMISE

7-17-2022 8:00p.m. to 8:30p.m.

Happenings occur when they seem least likely. The doors of churches are pushing open to be enveloped in the truths they have professed without living their actions for so long. Once I sat in the stillness of sanctuaries, seeking beyond the hidden cloaked statues of Our Lady. She has transformed over the ages, coming in ways the people were willing to receive her, despite the limitations of the false laws of cathedrals. Her movements were documented. Sightings of her statues taking life into her forms were recorded. Her presence was known, yet her voice was kept silent to those who spoke lies. Her beauty always resonated from her soul, emanating the warm glow of a tender, ethereal Mother, for she was and is Goddess Mother to all. In well-known shrines, they flocked to see her, witnessing permitted visions.

It was the children who were blessed with her messages of healing, of strength, and of prophecy. Such gifts were entrusted to the little ones, for in their innocence they are worthy of such trust.

Unknown to the masses, the incarnation of the Fae came into being in human form. Rulers of those dark times attempting to steal the Mother's wisdoms held them in secret caves to secure control over the populace. Wisdoms received by the children were recorded by those governing as the church. Often these little ones were whisked to convents.

It was there that strict directions to not speak of their interactions with the Lady were commanded. Through my invisible cloak, I witnessed and held fast to future resolutions.

I sat in the cauldron with both Fae and Our Mother, knowing what stew would bubble from it all, and I was grateful in knowing all along that the truth would surface and that the people would feast on a diet of sweet light, laced with heaven's promise.

MORGAN SHARES OF FAIRY AND TRUTH TALES

7-21-2022   12:20p.m. to 12:37p.m.

Fairy tales tell truths of many an ancient soul so that their memories would linger until they would resurrect. Here one finds giants, unicorns, mystical Pegasus, myths of the Gods and Goddesses, and the like.

I say to you, their tales have been altered and formed in such a way that the truth would be questioned. Yet, wise ones use these very same fables as doors to open and seek. Know that the imprint of truth will weave its messages as needed, in fable or in prophecy. Its Light will shine. Rather than call these fairy tales, I was known to call them truth tales. How I delighted in the surprise on the faces of the children while telling stories of my adventures with the Fae. I was good at weaving tales.

In telling a tale of a dragon and a unicorn, I received giggling applause from my sweet audience. When hearing how Pegasus flew to the ground to save a fear-filled babe from its burning barn, all were held spellbound. How we loved to spark the imagination of our little ones, so they could carry on our tales to the next generations. Some tales, though seeded by truth, became tall tales. How we feared what harm would come to the truth teller if they illuminated the dark with too much truth. Best to first open the hearts of the people, so they know the worth of love's magic.

MORGAN AND THE REVEAL

7-312022   4:47p.m. to 5:10p.m.

It is time to reveal secrets from days of yore. We, the high priestess sisters, sat in circles to open portals of creation to allow the womb energy of the Mother to flow through us. This was to expand into the nature kingdoms so that many a doorway would create its own dimension as its light would allow.

Encoded information was inscripted in writings and in the Christian bible later. How things would be interpreted would be according to the reader. When the Mother had a preference of which wisdoms must be preserved, designated locations were assigned to assist where the imprinting would occur. The caves, valleys, forests, and dried hidden waterways were all to tell of Her story. Many tellings have been revealed, and many more are to come, some surprising even the greatest of your scholars.

Locations house Orbs that fly across the lands. They hold the honor of activating the sacred symbols carved into her body. Their purposeful flights are filled with joy.

During such times, rumblings and quakes occur, moving Mother Gaia's templates into position, renewing her commitment to her ascension. People mirroring creation ascend with her or fulfill the prophecy of times of rendering, with many are leaving the planet.

With all being connected, an occurrence will cause effects for all. If you are knowing and living this, the time for suffering is at end. For fear shall no longer be your guide. Nay, you will live in rhythm with the Mother's soul, and trust that She knows the beginning and end times and finds Her freedom outside of time, where fear is no more and there is only love.

MORGAN SPEAKS OF MAAT'S JUSTICE

8-8-2022   10:55 p.m. to 11:20 p.m.

I tarry not over the spoils of man. That which has been denigrated has become chow for swine. I walked avenues where soldiers were once men of honorable intent. Now, I find spaces burnt in senseless battle. The land, the Earth—She is our cherished home. As those of tortured needs create battles of greed, the mighty sword of plenty swoops down as the Phoenix arises from the ashes.

My solace is found within my own knowing. Witnessing doesn't call me a victim. Rather, it yields from me mirrors of my inner truth. In days of old, justice was called Maat. Her scales held balance so acute, that her feather would cause the scales to tip with barely a weight of any substance. Her ways were quick and true. I stand not merely in balance but as the scale of balance in these times. The very cauldron or womb of creation that is feared by many is the home where I reside as this balance. My essence is a light of truth. I hold this with love for all. I am one who many weep after. In the depths of the sleeper's sorrow, they seek freedom from this separation of illusion. Being the Light from the cauldron, I am called to shine in such places. Each crack repaired by the compassion of Light; each piece brought together in a beautiful mosaic mural that has a space for every individual's work of art.

MORGAN WHISPERS

8-29-2022   9:22p.m. to 10:07p.m.

Breaking free from fear's chains, I no longer reside in the darkness of any vilification. I required that I remembered, myself! I came to the memory of the Divine within. There, I found no one to fear in the darkness or void. Nay, I did not. I remain sure-footed in my knowing myself as light. Please no longer pause in self-forgetting. While you may lollygag in your own darkness, I know of the light that remains hidden from you, due to your self-distraction. There in the void, I whisper memories from realms where we remain connected to each other. You may sense me. Others hear tales of long-gone days, that trigger memories. As the truth has called forth concealed myths, lies have come to the surface to be dissolved. And the truth lives.

At last, as has been told, "The truth shall set ye free." We are meeting, greeting, and dancing in the Memory of Oneness once more. The End and the Beginning!

About the Author

Joy Regina Melchezidek resides in a quaint, magical, little town in Pennsylvania. Filled with portals, ghost, fairy children, talking trees and whispering streams, she has called this place home for over 20 years. Along with writing, working as a child and peace advocate, she offers heart and soul classes, sessions, and lectures. Joy and Morgan La Fey also work together to bring through Channeled Soul Readings, Paralleling Life Readings and Fairy Classes. In her travels, you will find Joy fluttering around, connecting and loving the whole of humanity everywhere she goes.

To contact Joy for information on specific services, make an appointment or request speaking engagements call: 717-439-8842, between noon and 5:00p.m. EST. Email her at joyofunion@hotmail.com or message her on Facebook.

Made in the USA
Middletown, DE
13 April 2023

28749661R00142